Financial Management in Human Services

Marvin Feit, PhD
Peter Li, DSW

Financial Management in Human Services

Pre-publication
REVIEWS,
COMMENTARIES,
EVALUATIONS . . .

"**T**his text presents a practical overview of the 'nuts and bolts' of financial management in human services today. It is both timely and topical for students and practitioners working in this field. A number of field-tested forms are used throughout that are easy to understand and use. The attention to unit cost analysis and computerization is very insightful, analytic, and impressive. I regard this as must reading for anyone who needs to know how dollars and cents are linked to the services we deliver."

Michael J. Holosko, PhD
Professor, School of Social Work,
University of Windsor,
Windsor, Ontario, Canada

"**F**inancial Management in Human Services is a welcome addition to the field of human services. It is an excellent text that elucidates financial management from A to Z. In this age of accountability it should be required reading for all MSW students. It is an excellent amalgamation of theoretical and practical knowledge. This is a timely text that is urgently needed by the field."

John S. Wodarski, PhD
Janet B. Wattles Research
Professor and Director,
Doctoral Program and Research Center,
School of Social Work,
State University of New York
at Buffalo

The Haworth Press, Inc.

Financial Management in Human Services

Marvin Feit, PhD
Peter Li, DSW

The Haworth Press
New York • London

The Haworth Press, Inc., 10 Alice Street, Binghamton, NY 13904-1580

Cover design by Monica L. Seifert.

Library of Congress Cataloging-in-Publication Data

Feit, Marvin D.
    Financial management in human services / Marvin Feit, Peter Li.
        p.   cm.
    Includes bibliographical references and index.
    ISBN 0-7890-0569-7 (alk. paper)
    1. Human services—Finance. 2. Social service—Finance. 3. Social work administration.
I. Li, Peter. II. Title.
HV41.F375 1998
361'.0068—dc21   97-51449
                                                                                                              CIP

CONTENTS

ABOUT THE AUTHORS

Marvin D. Feit, PhD, is Professor and Director of the School of Social Work at the University of Akron, Ohio. The author or co-author of several books, he has written many articles and chapters in the areas of administration, financial management, substance abuse, health, and practice. Dr. Feit has made numerous presentations at national, state, and local conferences and has served as a consultant to profit and nonprofit organizations, federal and state government agencies, and numerous community-based agencies. Dr. Feit is a founding editor of the *Journal of Health and Social Policy* and the *Journal of Human Behavior in the Social Environment* (both published by The Haworth Press, Inc.).

Peter Kwok Chei Li, DSW, is Assistant Professor in the School of Social Work at the University of Akron, Ohio. He previously spent four years in Hong Kong teaching at Hong Kong Polytechnic. Dr. Li has taught social administration and program evaluation and has practical administrative experience in his areas of specialty—child welfare and the elderly.

Introduction

THE NEED FOR FINANCIAL MANAGEMENT IN SOCIAL SERVICE AGENCIES

Increasingly, there is discussion about the need for *better administration in social service programs*. There is no doubt that better administration translates into a more stable workforce, greater productivity, better accountability both to those who subsidize social services and those who rely on such services, and greater adaptability to environmental changes and challenges. Are social service agencies poorly managed in general? In this book, we discuss some key issues in administering a social service program, including program goals and objectives, the limited role a program plays in the lives of the clients, the expectations placed upon social programs to alleviate social ills, and the differences in productivity measurement as perceived by a program's funders and by the service providers whom the program employs.

Chapter 1 provides a description of the historical development of financial management in the social services arena. This development was both slow and sporadic at times as there were enough legitimate concerns about how social programs can adequately be monitored when they: (1) deal with some undefined public concerns about social conditions, which are not encountered by any other types of programs; (2) are responsible for combating social ills that are exacerbated by external phenomena such as recessions, which may have an impact on the lives of the citizens and their families; (3) are asked to provide services such as counseling and group sessions for which quality of services takes precedence over the number of client-worker contacts, while being monitored for the actual number of services provided; and (4) are asked to deal with social problems that have become more complex and more deep-seated than what can be handled by short-term counseling. Based on these concerns, one can expect that a formula that equates dollars allocated to services offered, as in a cost-benefit analysis, raised not just concerns but also resentment.

It is not surprising that any fiscal control of the organization needs to address some administrative issues, such as: how fiscal control would assist administrators; whether there are concerns about resource allocation or case management; improving program planning; monitoring and supervising staff activities; evaluating services for clients; providing information for making administrative decisions; and facilitating more meaningful communications among staff members.

Chapter 1 also examines how financial management is impacted by the differences between *for-profit* and *nonprofit* organizations and, within the nonprofit sector, the differences between nonprofit organizations such as libraries and social service agencies.

Chapter 2 provides some guidelines for developing a *financial management framework*. This framework must be realistic both to the people who determine whether the program is performing as promised and to the service providers. We discuss the types of information that are useful to policymakers, who determine the future directions of a program, and the types of information that are supplied by service providers. It is our belief that if there are any financial implications of services and service provision, some common grounds for service monitoring should be established.

Chapters 3 through 6 examine the ways in which financial management is used in program planning, service monitoring, estimating service costs and unit costs, and setting service priorities in years to come. In other words, we establish how the financial management framework can be integrated with other management systems. Also discussed are the ways in which administrators can utilize the information generated from the Financial Management System (FMS) to support administrative functions such as forecasting and goal determination, organizing activities for staff, monitoring activity flow and service provision, planning services in accordance with the policies upon which the program was established, and reporting efforts expended and outcomes accomplished.

To be effective, administrators need to know two things. The first is what they must perform in their jobs to make the organization more effective. This is a question of task specification. In a systems perspective, administrators need to know about the different administrative subsystems that comprise the work of administration and how they are interrelated. The second aspect is an identification of the personnel who can carry out these tasks. This is a question of administrative functions.

UTILIZING FINANCIAL MANAGEMENT

In this book, we define financial management for social service agencies as administrative activities that can be represented by four administrative subsystems. Chapters 3 through 6 deal with these four major administrative subsystems, namely: *fiscal subsystem* (budgeting and accounting); *service coordination (and management control); program planning;* and *program evaluation.* Each of these four subsystems is examined in the following five areas: (1) a definition of each subsystem and an elaboration of the scope of activities covered in each subsystem; (2) concerns and cautions that administrators should consider in carrying out administrative functions relating to each subsystem; (3) the reasons why administrators dealing with financial management need to consider each of these administrative subsystems; (4) the types of information that must be provided to the FMS to be useful to administrators; and (5) steps that should be taken in order to carry out administrative functions relating to each subsystem.

In Chapter 3, the fiscal subsystem (budgeting and accounting) activities are defined as those that record, process, document, and report monies received, monies committed, expenditures and expenditures committed, services provided, and number of clients served. The creation of multiservice agencies and the increased complexity of clients' problems lead to difficulties in service coordination and program planning. Along with these difficulties, there are new challenges and greater opportunities for financial management. Greater opportunities exist because a multiservice agency has greater service coordination capacity than do separate program units from different agencies. Since there is usually an administrative body and one board of directors, department heads in a multiservice agency have common bosses. However, the obstacles created because of personal territorial rights or turf protection may be significant. We believe that administrators who are responsible for budgets that have high ratios of variable revenue/total revenue and variable expenditure/total expenditure have greater flexibility and power. The discretion endorsed by agency contributors gives administrators greater flexibility in allocating resources, which consequently provides administrators with more power. We also believe that not all budgets require a sophisticated, automated FMS. The extent to which revenues are not earmarked for particular purposes is significant in determining the appropriate accounting method, ranging from petty cash management to a simple ledger system to basic bookkeeping to financial management.

An FMS can enhance the fiscal subsystem by providing information on what can be expected in terms of types and amounts of future revenues and expenditures, types of services requested, and types of services offered.

In Chapter 4, service coordination activities are defined as those that deal with case management; transfer of case management activities; and staff supervision, orientation, and training. We include intra-agency, interunit, and interagency activities and program-related and case-related activities. Service coordination is rendered more difficult by virtue of the trend toward multiservice agencies with specialized units, each unit having its own agenda and independent budget.

The interplay between the FMS and service coordination involves an examination of incidents where workers are spending time negotiating with other service providers for services to clients, or providing services which are of interest to few clients. Administrators would benefit from the FMS's ability to generate information about areas that require too much staff time in service coordination, thereby reducing the time that such workers have to work directly with clients. Unit cost analysis provides valuable information allowing administrators, supervisors, and staff to make wise decisions based on actual monetary information.

In Chapter 5, program planning activities are described as those that set and define goals and directions of an organization; establish standards for organizational performance; manage people based on results; and coordinate services and programs with other organizations. Some social service organizations have broad and unspecified goals so that program activities can be interpreted with as much flexibility as possible. Among the reasons for this lack of specificity is that programs were established as a result of policy initiatives undertaken by policymakers in one location, such as Washington, DC, while implementation of the policy initiatives was delegated to local offices; a decentralized service delivery model was favored to permit maximum flexibility and diversity. This mode of operation does not fare well with greater specificity and standardization. In addition, some programs, especially community-based or preventive programs, are meant to provide services to anyone who needs them in a community. Programs that are set up to address the diversified needs of diversified groups require innovation more than rigid goals. Furthermore, some programs have goals that have not been revised since their establishment decades ago; as time passes, some of these program goals become obsolete.

Chapter 5 also discusses how financial management can contribute in the area of program planning by addressing what we can expect to receive in monetary terms in the future; the types of services that are less time and effort consuming; the types of service demands projected; and changing client characteristics and service utilization patterns. This information would assist administrators in identifying areas in which program efforts should be allocated, and the types of services that will meet the objectives of the organization.

In Chapter 6, the focus in program evaluation is whether programs are meeting their objectives in an efficient manner. The criteria used in program assessment must be chosen carefully because different programs may be at different stages in their development. Based on the different program stages, different sets of program indicators should be used. When we focus on measurement issues related to program evaluation, we must be aware of the fact that concepts such as benefits, the beneficiaries of such services, the head count of program participants, the tangible and intangible services, and the benefits measured in monetary terms and social benefits must be addressed and carefully chosen in deriving a cost benefit analysis.

In program evaluation, one is examining issues related to a decision to increase, decrease, or maintain a service, or to eliminate it. In this context, concepts of effectiveness and efficiency become prominent. Effectiveness raises the issue of whether the services provided actually help the clients that these programs are targeted to serve. Efficiency focuses on whether the same types of services can be offered at a cost lower than the current cost for provision of such services.

Chapter 7 details the computerization of financial management. We believe that social service programs need to explore how to expedite services and establish service criteria that are understandable to funders, to the service providers, to the clients, and to the larger society. In order to satisfy the demands and requests from these parties, information should be readily available in two sets. The first set of information is service inquiry, such as service revenue, service utilization, and service costs with documentation. The second set of information is agency reports. In social service agencies, expenditures in the absence of units of services provided and number of clients served (whether clients are considered individuals or their family units) are not reflective of the agency's operations or of its impact on clients.

Also in Chapter 7, we suggest ways in which an agency's financial system can be computerized to monitor and analyze such factors as its service encounters, member activities or tasks, certain worker efforts, and client characteristics, so as to relate client needs and agency services. Basic reports and inquiries that can be generated to substantiate agency expenditures and to provide valuable information upon which administrative decisions can be based will be presented.

In order to have an FMS that produces reliable and accurate information, at least three information processing issues must be addressed. The first pertains to how current the information is, which affects the updating capacity of the system. The more updated the information, the better the system for making decisions. Information updating is expensive; thus, what data needs to be updated and how often are important considerations. The second issue is the identification of the persons or the units responsible for providing the information. If this task is not done well, one cannot identify the parties that are responsible for providing the information in an accurate and timely manner. The third issue is the identification of the users of the information. Information dissemination is a political process that also includes confidentiality and security issues. These three issues are incorporated in each of the four major administrative subsystems discussed in Chapters 3 through 6.

1. For example, in budgeting (in the fiscal subsystem), one is dealing with both program-related and case-related information. However, one also needs to know the type of staff who provide the services and the number of times services are used by participants, for the purpose of determining a cost for a unit of service. Supervisors and service providers are held responsible for furnishing this type of information to the FMS. Supervisors and management personnel who are in positions of allocating resources are the likely users of the information generated from this administrative subsystem.

2. In service coordination, we are dealing with current case-related information. It is helpful to know the supervisory structure and procedures for assigning workers to deal with individuals. Changes in the life of a client and/or a client's family, as well as changes in service demands, are important data which need to be kept current. Service providers and their supervisors are typically the key providers of this information. Because information is generated pertaining to workload and case management and case coordination, service providers and their supervisors are the logical users. Also, because of client confidentiality, there should be a distinction between program-related and case-related information.

3. In program planning, we are dealing with forecasting information. We want to know what we have, what we can anticipate in the near future, and what areas of change can be expected in the organization. In short, we need historical information and longitudinal analysis on revenues, expenditures, and services. We identify the service providers and their supervisors as the key parties in information provision. Because information is generated pertaining to caseload and case coordination, service providers and their supervisors are the logical users. Again, client confidentiality requires a distinction between program-related and case-related information.

4. In program evaluation, we need both program-related and case-related information. We also need to assess whether services are being offered to the right clients and by qualified personnel. We need to assess the ways in which cases are managed and assigned. The computation of cases and caseloads, and the incorporation of clients in case planning activities, should be reflected in this system. Current information may not be all that vital. Standardization of some of the methods of case coordination, worker performance, and agency operations is needed. We identify the service providers and their supervisors as the key parties in information provision. Because information is generated pertaining to caseload and case coordination, service providers and their supervisors are the logical users. And once again, client confidentiality requires a distinction between program-related and case-related information.

Finally, we raise a couple of issues in computer implementation related to each of the four administrative subsystems. The first issue is staff involvement. We identified earlier both the information providers and information users of each of these four subsystems. Here, we are referring to the politics of designing, modifying, and implementing the FMS. One important issue is the nature of activities involved in each of these subsystems. The nature of activities may determine the degree of standardization that administrators can impose on staff of the organization. The feasibility of designing a computerized system depends on the degree of standardization.

Chapter 1

Financial Management in Social Service Agencies

In this chapter, our focus is on whether the financial management of social service agencies should be scrutinized in the same manner as business organizations or other nonprofit organizations. We begin by looking at what distinguishes the financial management of nonprofit organizations from that of profit organizations. We then draw distinctions between nonprofit organizations, in general, and social service agencies as a subgroup of nonprofit organizations. This chapter concludes with a discussion of financial management as it pertains to social service agencies.

HISTORY OF FINANCIAL MANAGEMENT IN SOCIAL SERVICE ORGANIZATIONS

An examination of the historical development of nonprofit organizations in the United States reveals two trends. One is the ballooning of the funds allocated to the nonprofit sector; the other is the call for better financial scrutiny. These two trends suggest that administrators of nonprofit organizations must pay closer attention to fiscal accountability in the utilization of their resources and must develop a more careful scheme of resource allocation in a resource-scarce environment.

Nonprofit Organizations Are Big Business

With the push for greater focus on the fund-raising arena, philanthropists such as Carnegie and Rockefeller turned fund-raising into an art and a business. Block (1990, p. 55) noted that in 1984, the nonprofit sector received $68 billion from private contributions.

The federal revenue for that year was $666 billion while that year's gross domestic product (GDP) was $3,777 billion (U.S. House of Representatives, 1992). Big revenues and generous donations lead to a need for better fund management. The rise of federated organizations results in a higher demand for such an operation. This is accompanied by greater scrutiny of administrative functions, such as a greater justification of the sources of funds, the purposes for which funds are received, and how funds are earmarked for use. There is a demand for more sophisticated fiscal management, which includes a more complex accounting system that documents the correspondence between revenues and expenditures. There is a greater need for a more careful scheme of planning activities, which signifies how resources should be allocated. There is also a need to examine the internal management control issues, including where resources—such as staff time, funds, and use of facilities—are dispensed. There is a concern for reexamining whether the resources allocated are indeed generating the types of results that are desired.

According to Filer (1990), 10 percent of service workers are employed by nonprofit organizations, one out of six professional workers is employed by a nonprofit organization, and more than 10 percent of all property is owned by voluntary organizations. However, social welfare organizations receive roughly 40 percent of what is received by religious organizations. Their revenues from contributions lag behind those received by their educational counterparts.

Nonprofit Organizations Have Social Responsibilities

Nonprofit organizations receive monies from public agencies as well as from private donations. Organizations that meet the requirements of Section 501(c)(3) of the Internal Revenue Code have tax-exempt status. Because of this tax-exempt status, these nonprofit organizations are committed to organize their activities in a manner to attain the mission of the organization. But what is the mission of an organization? The fulfillment of a social responsibility may not fit into the scheme of business initiative. Some of the activities found in a social service organization may indeed be characterized as labor intensive, yielding low returns, and generating little public support. An example of these activities would be the training of "employment unready" welfare mothers.

The Era of Public Accountability

Filer (1990) pointed out that accountability should be focused on three major areas. The first is finances. This is a question of fiscal accountability. Administrators need to report what revenues are being generated and how these revenues are expended over a specific period of time. The second is in the area of programs. In this respect, administrators need to report what services, which client groups, and how much staff time and program expenditures are deposited in a particular area. This is not a question of how much money has been spent and in what areas. This is a question of service utilization and an assessment of the extent of program costs with respect to different groups of clients and different types of services. The third area identified by Filer is priorities. In this respect, administrators need to identify service goals and program objectives. These goals and objectives would then be used at the end of the fiscal cycle in measurement of program success. A greater need for accountability translates into a need for a better accounting system which identifies where monies collected from either public agencies or private donors are spent. It is also a question of having administrators determine with as much public endorsement as possible (1) what services should be identified, and (2) what activities of the organization should be monitored in accordance with program goals and objectives.

Feit (1979) notes that nonprofit organizations have moved from receiving grants from the government to receiving contracts from the government. Feit cites that there is a need to differentiate between contracts and grants. A contract is basically a statement used to procure research or services, whereas a grant is a mechanism to support research or services. A contract is a legal agreement between two or more parties and is used to purchase an identified set of services or a defined product under specific conditions. A grant, on the other hand, is awarded by a funding source and generally supports ideas generated from the field. It offers greater flexibility and is used more to support basic research, where the researcher is concerned primarily with gaining a fuller knowledge of the idea under study and contributing to scientific knowledge.

Social welfare programs began to rely on public monies as an organizational funding source. Filer (1990, p. 74) noted that the dependence on public monies led to greater constraints on the activities of the organizations.

Organizations need to adapt to the demands from the funding sources. There are areas in which organizations must develop to combat the greater public scrutiny, including keeping better accounts of any transactions of value in an organization. The assurance that dollars received and dollars spent are well documented is one way to combat such public scrutiny. The identification of community and client needs helps in goal setting. This activity sets the goals and mission of an organization. Furthermore, the exploration of the service needs and service gaps is a responsibility that a nonprofit organization is obligated to perform. The activities of a nonprofit organization are undergoing greater public scrutiny because of tax-exempt status, reliance on government monies, and social responsibility status.

Filer (1990, p. 77) further identified that nonprofit organizations have the responsibility of identifying and responding to the changing social needs of the society.

DEVELOPMENT OF FINANCIAL MANAGEMENT SYSTEMS IN SOCIAL SERVICE AGENCIES

In examining the development of financial management in social service agencies, it must be concluded that this is one aspect that has not been focused upon to the extent of other aspects of administration, such as program planning, service coordination, or program evaluation. What are some of the reasons behind the slow development of financial management in the social service sector? It was noted by Grubert in 1973 that social services were traditionally funded for carrying out the function of a program (Altshuler and Grubert 1996); the number of clients reached, the number of service units offered, and whether those services made an impact on the lives of the clients were not questioned. When a tighter accounting system was requested, the design called for a system that accounts for efforts, such as staff time expended by the agency, and measurement of the extent to which the lives of the clients are benefited. In short, the system must account for not only the dollars and time spent on a client, but also for the degree of improved functioning of the clients, whether it is individual functioning, family functioning, or community functioning.

The fact that grants rather than contracts were given to nonprofit organizations came under greater public scrutiny in the Nixon years. The provision of block grants from the federal government to the state governments was an indication that the program monitoring responsibilities had shifted from the federal agencies to the state offices. This shift of program initiatives is healthy as long as the state offices can assume such responsibilities. In other words, this shift of responsibilities requires that state offices assume the same types of social responsibilities as were intended for federal agencies. Another assumption is that, on the local level, communities are eager to offer services to vulnerable citizens even though some of them might not be rooted in the local communities. This is one important consideration as workers in contemporary America have been subjected to socioeconomic changes and geographic relocations caused by corporate restructurings through downsizing and mergers. Therefore, the role of carrying out social responsibilities looms larger for nonprofit organizations. Public scrutiny is no longer focused solely on funds dispersions. Public scrutiny places more attention on the tasks performed by nonprofit organizations, and on the extent to which social ills are alleviated among the populations that these organizations intend to serve.

IMPACT ON ADMINISTRATIVE DECISIONS AND OPERATIONS

A Useful Accounting System for Social Service Agencies

From the historical development of the program budgeting and monitoring of nonprofit organizations, it is evident that although the need for greater public scrutiny is felt, the mechanism for doing it has not been successfully developed. One has to ask how a nonprofit organization can fulfill its social responsibility and manage its funds in a responsible manner. One area that must be addressed is that administrators must plan services according to the needs of the clients. This is service planning. The second area is that staff time should be allocated to the areas in which resources should be deposited to address clients' needs. This is internal control and service coordination. The third area is that funds should be monitored with reports on income, revenues, and expenditures. This is fiscal management. The fourth area is that some corrective mechanisms must be installed to ensure that program costs, clients receiving services, and funds spent are conducted in an effective and an efficient manner. This is program evaluation. These four areas constitute the administrative subsystems that interact with the financial management system.

Financial Management Goes Beyond Accounting

Feit (1979) examined the functions of budgeting. A budget is an organizational plan of financial action. It performs two basic functions. First, it identifies in monetary terms the direction of the program and is based on clear objectives emerging from the planning process. Second, budgets are excellent tools to monitor the financial activities throughout the year. According to Feit (1979), the functions of an FMS are: "A generic financial management system might include and relate the organizational factors of identifying each service offered to clients, the manpower needs of each service, identification of actual cost in the traditional categories of consultant services, travel, space and utilities, consumable supplies, rental or lease of equipment, etc., in relation to each service, and the output measures for each service" (p. 95).

An accounting system that is useful to social workers and administrators of a social service program should be able to (1) properly reflect the work of the social workers, (2) provide useful information to policymakers, administrators, and social workers in setting goals for the organization, and (3) provide information on how the agency impacts on the functioning of individual clients, their families, and the community.

If this is a useful system, it should capture information on individual cases, on services to individual client systems, and on the functioning of the individual client system. Aggregate data, such as the number of cases handled and the number of group sessions held, may be reflective of some of the activities in service delivery. It does not capture the extent of program impacts on clients. The information captured in the accounting system in the 1970s was limited to counting and categorizing clients' contacts. The first attempt to incorporate case information into an administrative system was initiated by the Community Service Administration in 1966. During the early part of the 1970s, a goal-oriented social service delivery system was implemented. The emphasis was on the accountability of service outcomes being shared by both frontline service workers and agency management.

The right direction, as suggested by Altshuler and Grubert (1996), is to design an accounting system for social service agencies which captures unit cost. The need to operationalize and partialize types of services is well stated by Altshuler and Grubert (1996). The first mission is to define one unit of service as specifically as possible. The second mission is to specify tasks at each stage of the helping process. Unless a service can be partialized to a point where one can pinpoint what can be expected out of a helping process, one would have difficulty in monitoring its activities. Unless a process can define in specific terms what tasks are to be performed, the "unit" of service may be hard to determine. In the absence of a clear definition of what a "unit" of a particular service is, one has problems in talking about accomplishments or the time and effort needed to accomplish that service.

Specificity About the Goals of a Social Service Agency

In order to answer the question of whether one can be specific about the goals of a social service agency, one must examine the policies that were legislated to set up such a social service program. Some policies have a broader mission than others. For example, if a neighborhood center is set up to empower the community, administrators of such a program may have difficulty in partializing the tasks that would empower the community, or in defining the indicators used in the measurement of community empowerment. However, administrators of a service such as child day care may have fewer difficulties in defining the types of care that workers provide for the children in care, or in specifying the number of hours of care each child received in a day, in a week, or in a specific period of time.

One major problem in specifying the goals of some social service programs is that some programs are charged with the mission of alleviating a particular social problem. Newman and Turem (1974) pointed out that the social responsibility of alleviating these social problems may be a tall order for some administrators. One must realistically ask whether some of these social problems are similar in magnitude and in degree of severity to those which these programs were established to combat.

For accountability to be meaningful, Newman and Turem (1974) stated that the following conditions need to be met: that professional and technical work can be provided if the society makes the resources available; that this work will be provided in the manner promised; and that the problem may then be effectively minimized at the smallest possible social cost.

The usefulness of unit cost analysis is that it provides a common ground for policymakers (such as boards of directors, administrators, and social workers) to examine the appropriateness of services provided, the appropriateness of contracting services out to private agencies, and the appropriateness of assigning professional or nonprofessional workers to direct services (such as counseling) and indirect services (such as planning and administering services).

Current Interplay Between Financial Management and Social Service Organizations

The lack of a better FMS to date stems from the difficulties in identifying program goals that can fully reflect the work of a social service organization. As Newman and Turem (1974) suggested, the promotion of a sound FMS was not met with real challenges. The first reason is the lack of evidence that direct services, such as counseling, lead to improvement of client functioning. The second reason is the absence of a monitoring system by which the federal or the state government involved can assess program evaluation.

One of the major criticisms made by Henderson, Trennepoli, and Wert (1984) concerning the issue of accountability is the political context under which accountability is defined. The accountability issue was viewed as providing a rational basis for funds allocation.

Henderson and colleagues (1984) suggested that it is not what decisions are made, but rather the way decisions are made that should be of primary concern. The types of decisions that are made include: (1) those regarding fiscal and human resources; (2) who has a right to what share of the resources; and (3) what goals ought to be set.

QUESTIONS OF COSTS AND BENEFITS

Distinguishing Aspects of Financial Data in Nonprofit Organizations

Contributions

Contributions to a nonprofit organization are tax exempt to the donor if the organization has filed for tax-exempt status with the Internal Revenue Service. Some contributions may be made without any specific instructions about their applications, while others may have criteria to be met before expenditures can appear on a balance sheet.

Dividends

It was found that in a nonprofit organization, administrators do not need to report the dividends or other agency-related investments (Antony 1987, p. 77). This does not mean that agencies do not need to keep track of monies they receive, such as dividends or other investments. It means that they do not need to put those types of transactions into their ledger systems.

Types of Contributions

Antony suggested that contributions received in a nonprofit agency should be handled with care. There are some scenarios that may prove to be complicated for accountants. One type of complication comes from "contributions received in one period of time [for] which use is restricted to a later period" (Antony 1987, p. 79). In this respect, the accounting must reflect that revenues may be received in a particular year and that the related expenditures are to occur in the following years. Other types of contributions are those made for the use of some operating activities. For example, gifts donated to senior citizen centers for Christmas or birthday presents can be used only for those purposes. Antony further pointed out that "the laws of all fifty states require nonprofit organizations to separate endowment assets from operating assets. Such a separation is, in any case, obviously essential in judging an organization's ability to meet its operating financial needs" (Antony 1987, p. 79).

Financial Balancing

It is good for the morale of business organizations to report windfall profits since such profits are a reflection of good performance. In a nonprofit agency, unused revenues indicate that either the agency requested a bigger budget than needed, or that something was wrong with the program resulting in nonperformance. "A non-business entity measures its financial performance by the extent to which its net income is approximately zero" (Antony 1987, p. 77).

A Comparison Between Social Service Agencies and Other Nonprofit Organizations

Public Control Over Services Provided

Since nonprofit organizations are established for the purpose of providing services to certain segments of the public, then, in a sense, the general public can be considered the consumer of these products. For example, a library is established to serve the public's interests. As a result, there is an issue of public accountability. Furthermore, the public or the taxpayers can dictate the types of books on display, the types of people for whom the library is established, and even the social behavior of the key participants, including the service providers and the consumers. In this respect, the services provided are very much tied into the demands of the general public.

In many ways, a social service organization also responds to the public's demands in its operations. For example, a community-based social service agency such as a neighborhood center or a senior citizen center is charged with the responsibility of taking care of some of the vulnerable members of a particular community. In the case of a senior citizen center, it is more than a place for senior citizens to eat. It is also a place of socialization for those whose social network is small; it is a place for them to find out about the changes in policies that may affect their Medicare benefits, their half-fare transportation tickets, etc. In other words, it is usually set up with the purpose of assisting senior citizens of a particular locality in more than one aspect of their lives.

The client group of a seniors center, as prescribed by laws and regulations, is composed of persons who have attained a particular age. The localities of particular centers are accessible to particular groups of senior citizens are also dictated by distinct service areas, thereby giving administrators the authority to exclude senior citizens from other communities. The types of services are mostly prescribed, such as meals and recreational programs. Most senior citizens will use their discretionary power to obtain other services in health, education, and service applications.

Even though the public, or sectors of the public, are the recipients of social services, the service recipients cannot dictate the parameters of service provision because service planning cannot be performed in a vacuum. After all, taking on more responsibility to provide more services can be discussed, but expansion of services or service areas costs money. Most senior citizen centers are staffed with only one program director, one full-time social worker, and many support staff, including a chef, meal attendants, and volunteers. The wish for expansion may be there but the money is not.

Furthermore, one must ask whether the center is in a better position if it is patronized by many people. There is no clear answer to this question. Simply put, the amount of funds available for such a center is not contingent upon the number of participants. The amount of funds available may hinge on whether the political backing of supporters of such centers in a community is strong or stronger than those of other competitors for the funds. In this sense, the rational view of getting appropriate funds may count less than other considerations, such as the political agenda of the policymakers.

Support for Programs

Nonprofit organizations such as libraries, parks, zoos, and museums are likely to receive general support because such organizations provide services that are considered beneficial to all members of the public, with few, if any, adverse consequences.

Conversely, social service programs in which social workers are often employed are established to serve specific needs with respect to populations and problems. These include programs for the homeless, for children in foster care systems, for gay and lesbian youths, and for the mentally disabled. Social service programs are set up to protect the rights of these vulnerable clients. Administrators of homeless programs have a difficult time in finding locations in which they can provide nighttime shelters for individuals or families; administrators of group homes for foster care adolescents, or halfway houses for former mental patients, encounter comparable problems. Providers of services to people whose sexual orientations or ailments may gain little sympathy from the public at large may experience a lack of unilateral public endorsement of their organizations.

It is common for critics of social service programs to talk about programs not meeting service goals or objectives. A nighttime shelter for homeless people is a temporary place to "house" these individuals. Sometimes these shelters are organized so that children of the homeless need to be "placed" away from their mothers. This program "houses" homeless individuals; it is not a housing program. It does not provide a solution for the individuals. Such a program is often referred to as a nighttime shelter because participants are being "bused in" and "bused out" of these shelters at off hours so that the tranquility of a neighborhood can be maintained. Thus, a shelter is quite different from other nonprofit programs such as an opera house, museum, park, or public library. In a consumer satisfaction survey, there is reason to believe that many social service agencies would not score high. If the measure of success is service utilization, can we not say that the success of such a social intervention would be the elimination of homelessness as a problem in our society?

Beneficiaries of Nonprofit Organizations

A library is a public service deemed useful to everyone in a community. Military defense is a public service that everyone agrees is needed to safeguard national security, thereby benefiting local communities. Defense is a public good because its purpose is to protect all members of a nation; libraries are available to all and tailored to local needs.

In the formation of some social service programs, the public has been faced with social problems that needed to be addressed; the extent of the problems, the ways of remedying them, and the people who were to be covered by such remedies were unknown. Some members of the public might have forgotten that such services, in addition to benefiting the service recipients, also benefit the public at large. For example, services to the elderly are a public commitment made to ensure that elderly citizens receive support that enhances their lives over and above providing pensions and supplementary income. Benefits include emotional comfort to family members of the elderly, in addition to the physical and emotional support provided directly to elderly persons.

However, a more narrow view that is often taken is that the direct recipients of these social service programs are the only beneficiaries of such programs. By the mere fact that we are dealing with the public good, it must be assumed that such services benefit the public at large. In a way, when examining services provided by neighborhood community centers in places such as Chicago and New York in the 1960s, it can be understood that these services were meant for the society at large. Some of these programs were established in an effort to maintain social harmony.

In short, while there is consensus about who the beneficiaries are of nonprofit organizations such as libraries, such consensus does not exist when the focus changes to social service agencies.

BUDGETARY MODIFICATIONS FOR SOCIAL SERVICE AGENCIES

In the earlier part of this chapter, we explored some of the differences in operations among the various nonprofit organizations. Since the operations are different, can we expect a traditional form of accounting to be applicable to nonprofit organizations such as libraries and social service agencies? The answer is maybe. With appropriate modifications, the accounting systems for social service agencies can be made more appropriate.

We must understand the operations of these programs. Historically speaking, many of these community-based social service programs were established as a result of President Johnson's War on Poverty. Whether poverty can be eradicated cannot hinge entirely on efforts expended by these programs. We know that many of the benefits, such as public assistance, Aid to Families with Dependent Children (AFDC), Medicare, and Medicaid were enacted in an attempt, but not a coordinated effort, to stamp out poverty. Many senior citizens, for example, were probably assisted in moving above the threshold of poverty by a combination of their participation in senior citizen programs, the increase of Social Security benefits, and the comprehensive coverage of Medicare.

Within social service programs, a further distinction must be made between entitlement programs and direct services programs. The framework of financial management developed here will apply to the latter type of program.

Sometimes, there is a tendency to cluster programs together because they receive funding from the same source or from the same legislative acts. We realize that there are different types of agencies. Some provide certification services to clients. Some ensure that accurate direct payments to clients are made in a timely manner. Some explore with clients the types of conditions and problems encountered and work alongside their clients in finding ways for clients to function better in such situations, or in advocating institutional changes in policies or in programs.

Roughly, government offices (such as Medicaid) are classified as the types of agencies involved in certifying clients for services. For example, the Social Security Administration is primarily involved in ensuring that accurate monthly payments are made to the entitled citizens, and Family and Adult Services are involved in providing direct counseling services, information, and referrals to those who need them. Two issues stand out in this classification. The first is that the degree of intangible services provided by workers in these offices varies. The second is the degree of nonstandardization in case handling. These two issues affect the nature of work performed by staff members, the staffing pattern, and the expectations of program performance by clients. Financial management, being heavily invested in finding the means of providing better quality services with the minimum amount of resources, does have an interest in exploring how staff time is spent, who is being held responsible in providing services, and how much autonomy should be granted to staff in working out a problem-solving formula with clients.

As the ratio of the intangible/tangible service mix increases, the time spent by staff is also likely to increase. It is highly likely that better trained staff is allocated to deal with situations that call for professional judgment. When the degree of standardization is low, more autonomy must be granted to staff in handling these situations.

A few other points merit mention. First, the expenditure on social service agencies is probably at a minimum when compared with that of huge "entitlement programs" such as Social Security retirement benefits and Medicare. Second, if program effectiveness is ever applied to such entitlement programs, evaluators tend to analyze only who receives benefits, and whether there are individuals who are not entitled to benefits but who are, nonetheless, receiving them. The scrutiny of services provided by social service agencies is much more intense. Evaluators hold social service agencies responsible for dealing with social problems. The success of attaining this goal or mission, however, may have little to do with the way the programs are run; for example, if the provision of job training for people in preventive programs does not lead to employment, this may be more indicative of the economic reality than of underlying problems with the job training itself. Moreover, evaluators of social service programs tend not to inquire into whether such programs are being adequately funded to implement their service plans.

Nothing stated previously should be taken as a suggestion that we believe that social service agencies should not be held accountable for their services. The accounting system is designed to ensure that all public monies and private contributions are spent properly, with the right receipts. However, pitting accountability in the social service agency arena against service effectiveness or program efficiency measurements is a tall order. The correlation between account accuracy and service effectiveness may be a good idea, but this correlation may not be found in the existing audit system. Moreover, the concept of administrative efficiency may have limited application for a social service agency. Administrative efficiency can be attained if administrators have the power to restructure the workforce, to be selective in the assignment of tasks based on merit and capabilities, to recruit and fire staff based on merit and needs, to plan activities that result in greater productivity, and to select services that make the greatest impact on a selected group of clients. In a social service agency, administrators may be somewhat handicapped when they cannot restructure the work force. Some operations are structured to employ staff of different designated disciplines, and value conflicts may arise when there is no clearly defined authority structure among different groups of staff. The structure is determined more by personality than by organizational roles. The maintenance of the current power structure, turf protection, and discipline defenses seem to surpass in importance the attainment of the organizational mission.

Chapter 2

A Framework for a Financial Management System

FMS SUPPORTS
FOR ADMINISTRATIVE DECISIONS

To determine how an FMS provides administrative support, the following questions must be answered:

1. With what functions can the FMS support the four administrative subsystems, i.e., fiscal (budgeting and accounting), service coordination, program planning, and program evaluation?
2. How can these functions be carried out?
3. If these functions are implemented, how would these subsystems be supported?
4. What information is needed to carry out this implementation process?
5. In organizational activities, what corrective actions should be taken by administrators upon receiving feedback generated by the FMS?

Internal Control

In any organization, administrators need to examine challenges from the environment (whether to design better services for the community or for the public at large), and either to structure activities in ways to combat such challenges or to devise new strategies for turning challenges into opportunities for new ventures. Or, administrators may structure their organizations in a manner that permits staff size to grow. Administrators can make changes only in activities, such as restructuring teams and changing staff behavior. Most administrators are not in a position to impose changes upon the community or upon society at large. Some administrators may have better opportunities than others to work as partners of policy-makers who advocate for or implement policy changes.

Administrators must adapt to changes that occur in the organization, which may impact on one or more of the four areas in administration. For example, changes in the composition of the client group is one area that may cause an organization to revisit its own goals and start asking questions about whether the organization has arranged its activities in the best manner to move ahead in the future. This is a function of the program planning administrative subsystem. A second area that concerns administrators encompasses whether services are offered to clients in a timely fashion, why some services are better utilized than others, and whether too much money is spent on indirect costs (that is, monies spent in areas that support staff functions rather than in areas that provide services directly to the clients, including staff-client interaction, which is one form of services). All of these concerns are functions of service coordination. Any reduction of duplicative efforts would cut down staff time, which can be translated into cutting back of service costs. A third area that concerns administrators is how programs impact on the lives of clients. Administrators need to determine whether services offered by the organization are received in a timely manner by clients and whether services offered can affect the lives of clients in a positive sense. If services are appropriately offered and received and such services subsequently benefit the lives of clients, then services can be considered effective. If services are offered by fewer workers and are received by more clients, then services are being offered in an efficient manner. This is a function of program evaluation. In brief, we have identified functions by which fiscal management can provide valuable information to administrators so that they can design and structure work for their staff to accomplish goals of an organization; administrators can also make use of information from fiscal management to organize better methods for staff in orchestrating better services for their clients. Administrators can use unit costs to derive methods of measuring program costs for their clients. With this information, administrators can have better control of the organization by monitoring activities that work toward the accomplishment of agency goals and by organizing activities to provide services which can benefit more clients with fewer staff hours. Administrators can provide corrective actions once they identify which services are overutilized, underutilized, overstaffed, and understaffed. In brief, administrators would have better control of organizational activities under their jurisdictions by using the information that can be obtained from an FMS.

Financial Auditing

> The comprehensive audit . . . concentrates on the accounting and reporting system used by a particular agency and checks transactions selectively. The general audit examines the accounts of agency disbursing and certifying officers to determine the legality of each transaction. . . . The commercial audit is applied to government corporations and enterprises. (Ott 1993, p. 57)

Financial auditing is useful to an organization as it provides an objective assessment of the current operation of the organization, its policies and missions, and the types of corrective actions that need to be performed to meet goals and accomplish tasks.

Financial auditing should be a continuous process with as much input as possible from people who are involved in its operations. Unless the key parties are involved, financial auditing may be reduced to an exercise that will occur only on a semiannual or on an annual basis and, in such case, its impact will be greatly reduced.

The FMS that this book suggests incorporates fiscal management with case coordination, case monitoring, program planning, goal setting, and program evaluation. The rationale is that economic considerations for an operation must be viewed alongside the practice wisdom of the service providers and the relationship between the organization and the community it serves.

For financial auditing to be effective, the auditors must focus on the organization, its operations, its services, its clients, and the tasks that the organization plans to perform. Sometimes, auditors fail to detect problems because they fail to understand the business of the organization (Knox 1994, p. 128). Financial auditing in a nonprofit organization is likely to be different from one performed in a for-profit organization.

One key aspect of financial auditing is to verify that fund allocations are documented and authenticated properly. Another aspect is to ensure that parties receiving funds are separate from those who document expenditures so as to minimize the risks of funds misallocation and conflicts of interest. Financial auditing in a nonprofit organization is much more extensive than an examination of bookkeeping—it interprets financial transactions in relation to the stated policies and practices of an organization.

Since auditing is guided by the operational policies, guidelines, and procedures of the organization, it also provides an assessment of whether clients are provided with the correct services at the right time. It examines whether those who are assigned to assist clients are certified and trained. It assesses whether there are clear guidelines in funds allocation and bookkeeping.

In brief, financial auditing examines the appropriateness of program activities, the choice of clients, the adequacy of the maintenance of the facilities in which services are offered, the training and certification of service providers, the documentation of funds received and expenditures made, methods of funds payment, and the tracking of revenues and expenditures.

In the FMS, one can identify clients, staff time, facility usage, and direct and indirect costs in service provision as the major components. It provides a unit cost analysis in which different programs and different services can be compared and analyzed. The information generated by the FMS is similar to that needed by financial auditing.

Specific steps should be taken to ensure that the financial audit evaluates the actual operation of the organization. Before the audit occurs, the activities to be evaluated should be those agreed upon by the organization being audited, the organization that will make use of the audit, and the auditors. After agreeing upon what should be included in the audit, the auditors should spell out the exact procedures. Sometimes, auditors fail to identify the right parties for the right decisions (Knox 1994, p. 128).

Careful examination should be made of organizational activities such as documentation of monetary transactions, staff training records, equipment acquisition forms, facility inspection records, and services to clients. Such a selection of items should reflect actual agency operation. In that respect, items selected should be representative of items to be audited. Sometimes, random selection of cases is appropriate.

For the findings of the financial audit to be useful, a mechanism that permits organizations to make the appropriate changes and adaptations needs to be well implemented. For example, if it is found that services are being delivered to a majority type of clients, this finding should be utilized for future development and planning of programs. Or, if services are not addressing the needs of the community, this finding should be incorporated into the evaluative processes of the organization. Or, if documentation of funds is found to be inadequate, then a better ledger system with appropriate bookkeeping practices should be implemented. In other words, the findings of the financial audit should support administrators in making decisions in one or more of the administrative subsystems, namely fiscal management, service coordination, program planning, and program evaluation.

FMS SUPPORTS FOR ADMINISTRATIVE SUBSYSTEMS

Program Planning Supports

Forecasting is possibly one of the most important areas in which the FMS can provide program planning support. The FMS can provide information for preparing a budget to be presented to the board of directors for review and approval regarding the amounts of revenues that can be anticipated for the current year and in the forthcoming years, and what revenues have been received. In addition, administrators can obtain information on service-related types of planning based on what funds can be anticipated, what kind of personnel can be recruited or retained, and what service needs tend to be in greatest demand.

With this information, administrators can plan accordingly. One key element is who should be involved. It would be wise for administrators to involve people who are in positions to endorse the passing of budgets and the people who are involved in services provision. Those who need to review and endorse the budgets need to know what constraints there are if funds are not appropriated properly; those who provide services need to know the extent to which they can assist their clients. In brief, the implementation of program planning requires economic, political, and organizational considerations. In an economic sense, administrators need to know what funds are available, how funds can be appropriated, and the impact of funds allocation on service delivery. In the organizational context, administrators need to be concerned with including the operations of the organization. For administrators to make decisions on the organization, the operations of the existing service delivery system, such as the types of clients served and the types of services offered over the past years, need to be examined. Based upon the information on services and clients, administrators are in a better position to make projections in planning the types of services that best fit the needs of their clients in the future. The political aspect of service planning is that prioritization of services affects clients and workers. Because some workers may be asked to do more than others, issues of fairness and appropriate rewards require consideration.

Expected Outcomes

The financial information delineates limits on which services can be provided. It informs administrators about whether an organization will be in a growth or retrenchment phase. It sets limits on the expenditures permitted for categories of services, such as individual counseling sessions, and it establishes a plan for funds to be appropriated.

Informational Needs for Effective Program Planning

Administrators need to identify the types of services to be provided, the clients who will be receiving services, and the types of personnel needed for the provision of such services. In addition, unit cost analysis provides useful information about, for example, how much the organization is spending on the provision of a particular service.

Organizational Adaptations

Using information provided by the FMS, administrators can establish a platform of communication with other key participants, such as members of the board of directors, middle-line managers, frontline supervisors, or professional workers. Administrators can monitor organizational activities to ensure that funds are appropriated as anticipated and that services are delivered as planned.

Fiscal Management Supports

Budget preparation, auditing, and budget reconciliation are the primary fiscal support functions provided by the FMS. With the information provided, administrators can prepare a budgetary plan in terms of where resources are to be allocated. Again, it would be wise for administrators to involve people who are in positions to endorse the ways resources are to be allocated. Through negotiation, a rational basis can be determined for funds or resource allocation.

Expected Outcomes

The financial information provided by the FMS allows administrators to be accountable to the funders and board of directors for services and expenditures. It also allows administrators to derive a cost value for each unit of service provided. The unit cost analysis is, in a way, setting standards in monetary terms about how much it will cost an agency to provide one unit of a particular kind of service, such as home care. This standardization of services in monetary terms allows administrators to make interagency comparisons of the cost of funding a similar program.

Informational Needs for Effective Fiscal Management

To compute the unit cost for a particular type of service, administrators need information such as the number of clients served in each type of service (such as outreach) offered by the organization and the number of hours each staff member who is responsible for providing such services spends each week in delivering each type of service. The information enables the administrators to determine the number of units of services offered and the amount of money the organization has spent in the delivery of such services. The amount of money spent relies on direct costs, such as staff salary, and indirect costs, such as office rent, equipment rentals, etc. In addition, information is needed on revenues, which is comprised of funds committed to the organization by funding sources and projections based on funds raised in previous years.

Organizational Adaptations

In budget reconciliation, administrators need to determine which areas can spend more and which areas need to be confined as far as expenditures are concerned. In unit analysis, administrators can assess whether areas that are overfunded are fully justified in their expenditures, and in areas where resources are scarce, can make a determination of the consequence of clients having fewer services or no services.

Service Coordination Supports

The FMS provides the following service coordination supports:

1. Establishing financial constraints on service provisions. With information provided by the FMS, administrators can establish a rational negotiation process with staff members over the thorny issue of resource allocation. Even though the process encompasses personality issues and political agendas, the discussion should be focused on allocation of the available economic means.

2. Identifying staff accountability issues. Assigning staff to perform tasks is one of the most important functions of administration. Task assignment encompasses many different considerations, including staff qualifications, individual workloads, whether some staff members can work together, and whether the tasks assigned to particular staff members are interesting and foster their professional growth.

Although task assignment is an important consideration, so is financial accountability. At times, administrators need to review and analyze the amount of staff time spent in a particular service area or on a particular group of clients. Judgment calls need to be made, factoring in financial constraints and financial opportunities.

3. Determining service reporting needs. Practically everyone in an organization needs service reporting. Policymakers, such as members of the board of directors, need to know which services are being requested and which services are or are not being offered. The information provides an organization with a plan of action for the future, whether it involves service cutbacks, service expansion, or restructuring of the service delivery model.

Expected Outcomes

An effective service delivery model can be designed by implementing one of the following strategies: (1) formalizing methods of service coordination through automation; (2) contracting out services in an effort to lower the organizational liability issues; or (3) restructuring the workforce into autonomous teams within the organization to carry out organizational missions.

Informational Needs for Effective Service Coordination

To compute the unit cost for a particular type of service, administrators require information as to which workers are serving which clients. For better coordination, administrators need to know if services are offered to the clients in sequential order or in some orchestrated fashion. Administrators further need to know who is responsible for the provision of particular services. Based on this information, administrators should be able to determine whether the current service coordination method is cost efficient. Administrators can also work with staff members to determine if other less time-consuming service coordination can be formulated.

Organizational Adaptations

Any major changes in service coordination may affect one or more of the following areas: (1) organizational restructuring, such as merging certain service units, or reducing organizational efforts in a particular area (e.g., contracting services outside an organization); (2) expansion of service activities, such as seeking more collaboration from community agencies; (3) task restructuring, to assign more or less authority and responsibility to staff; and (4) centralization or decentralization of fiscal autonomy to the service units.

Program Evaluation Supports

Administrators can use the FMS for program evaluation support by examining one or more of the following areas:

1. Choice of evaluative criteria. In evaluating a social service program, overhead costs must be justified based on the stage of development (that is, the services presently being offered) of the current program. Normally, it may take considerable time and money to set up and develop a fully-functioning program. Some of the criteria that administrators need to examine include: the types of services needed by the target population; the types of supports received from the community in which the program is located; whether the current program is capable of providing the needed services; whether the current operation has a way to involve staff in setting program goals and service standards; and whether fiscal and service transactions are being reported in an accurate and timely manner.

2. Program costs. Administrators may need to determine if program costs are justified by the number of service units delivered to clients. A major concern would be whether too much money is spent on indirect costs, which are funds spent in areas apart from direct services to clients. Sometimes, a program may be operating in a manner in which the cost of service coordination exceeds the cost of services provided directly to clients. Consequently, administrators may need to revisit the procedures currently used by the agency in service coordination. The aim is to locate areas in which services are delayed or in which too much paperwork is involved. If such areas can be identified, administrators can then consult with responsible staff members in an attempt to devise a smoother operation. This may require fewer staff hours and fewer staff members, which will likely cost the program fewer dollars. This is one way to reduce the amount spent on indirect costs. Monies saved on indirect costs may be reallocated to areas that will benefit clients directly, such as program expansion which would provide more units of services to existing clients or provide services to a larger number of clients. An administrator would then need to consider whether the program is serving a large enough number of clients to justify the budgets appropriated for the program.

A ratio of direct service costs to indirect service costs provides an indication of where monies are spent. It probably is preferable to see a budget report in which monies are spent primarily on services to clients. After all, we mentioned earlier in this chapter that services are the output or product of a social service organization. Therefore, a higher direct-to-indirect costs ratio may be viewed favorably by the board of directors or by the public at large.

3. Client-requested services. Administrators may need to evaluate whether the agency is providing services that are requested by its clients. This is one area that administrators and service providers must examine with great caution. Some services, such as home care services for the elderly, are requested and welcomed by the elderly population suffering from particular physical disabilities. Conversely, some services, such as child welfare, are services that are not requested by clients (the agency is carrying out a mission designated by the public to protect vulnerable children).

4. Target population. Administrators may need to evaluate whether the client group designated to be assisted is actually obtaining the needed services. In a community-based preventive program, one may want to reach out to children who may be on the verge of substance abuse. The existence of the program may be welcomed by the community, especially in the form of after-school tutoring services. As time goes by, one realizes that the program has attracted children who are unlikely to fall into the category of substance abuse. Therefore, the preventive program may have reached out to a different group, and the original targeted group may remain unassisted.

Expected Outcomes

Resources such as staff time and facility usage can be evaluated as to the costs of providing services to clients. An identification of procedures that may be causing unnecessary service delays or consuming excessive staff time would lead to procedural changes, such as implementing office automation or restructuring staff, and would lower the costs of providing similar services. This would be a means of decreasing program costs and increasing program efficiency.

Identifying services not provided by the agency or not provided to some needy clients helps administrators to restructure some of their organizational activities, preferably involving consultations with staff members, to meet such a service demand. Making sure that services are received by the most needy group is a mission of the organization in carrying out its social responsibility, and is an important function of program evaluation. For a social service program to be effective, it must provide the needed services and ensure that such services are received by the most needy group of clients.

Informational Needs for Effective Program Evaluation

To compute the unit cost for a particular type of service, administrators require information on the number of staff hours spent in supervising subordinates, attending case conferences, making home visits, writing reports on cases, and contacting other service providers for service referrals or coordination of services. This information helps administrators to derive direct costs in providing a particular type of service. Administrators further examine how much time each type of service utilizes in common areas of expenses (such as the use of conference rooms and educational facilities and the number of Xerox copies made) to determine the indirect costs. With a clear count of heads, administrators can determine the unit costs of each type of service based on the amount of direct and indirect costs for each client.

Organizational Adaptations

Any major findings in the program evaluation exercise may lead to some revisitations and reexaminations of one or more of the following organizational activities: assigning staff to special teams; reestablishing the authority structure to ensure that proper supervision is made accessible to service providers; redesigning the forms and procedures for reporting; and reexamining the goals and missions of the organization. Some of these changes may affect the ways services are currently coordinated in the organization; some changes will impact on fiscal reports. In addition, some modifications may be necessary to reestablish the direction and position of the organization.

SUMMARY

In this chapter, a framework for a financial management system for social service agencies was proposed, which stressed the importance of viewing the FMS as the central function in relation to other administrative functions, such as planning for future activities or better services for clients; organizing staff in a manner that holds them responsible for the delivery of appropriate services in a timely fashion; monitoring staff activities so that public accountability of program funds and professional responsibility for agency activities can be attained; budgeting with an emphasis on having program costs and expenditures correspond with program revenues; and making forecasts of service utilization and program revenues so that staff stability and program growth can be achieved.

Chapter 3

The Fiscal Subsystem

PURPOSES AND FUNCTIONS OF THE FISCAL SUBSYSTEM

In this chapter, the fiscal subsystem is examined in relation to the overall financial management system. The fiscal subsystem reports on all income and expenditures. Based on how these reports are designed, the collected amounts and their uses can be determined in the following areas: (1) assessing changes in revenues, expenditures, and service utilization; (2) monitoring patterns in services and expenditures; (3) analyzing program costs and unit service costs; and (4) taking corrective management actions.

ACCOUNTING PRINCIPLES AND METHODS

There is no question that accounting principles must be adhered to in developing the FMS. Two concepts need to be elaborated: the first is a distinction between fixed and variable revenues and expenditures, and the second is a distinction between budgeting and financial management. Some social programs know that their budgets remain fairly constant from year to year, with slight modification in cost of living adjustments. This is fixed revenue. Additional revenues may be allocated as a result of donations, raffle ticket sales, etc. This type of revenue varies from year to year and constitutes variable revenue; in addition to being variable, some monies committed may not be collected. A program that is dictated to have five staff members at predetermined salaries can project how much monies would be spent on salaries. This is a fixed expenditure.

Activities such as "trips" are often subsidized by the program even though some of the participants are asked to make a contribution. Depending on the number of people who want such a service, the amount of subsidy varies. This is a variable expenditure. If administrators in a particular program—Program A—have a large budget, 50 percent of the revenues from contract monies and 50 percent from fund-raising, they would have more monies to spend on activities of their discretion. Administrators in another program—Program B—which, similarly, has a large budget, may have 90 percent of the revenues coming from contract monies and 10 percent from fund-raising; they would have fewer dollars to be spent at their discretion. Administrators in a third program—Program C—receive a small budget (say 10 percent of the total revenue of program A), with 50 percent of the monies coming from contract monies and 50 percent of the monies coming from fund-raising. These administrators have fewer dollars to spend at their discretion. Administrators in a fourth program—Program D—receive the same small budget as administrators in Program C, with 90 percent of the revenues coming from contract monies and 10 percent coming from fund-raising. These administrators have fewer dollars than their counterparts in Programs A and B. Even worse, they only have 10 percent of a small budget for discretionary use. We believe that the usefulness of the accounting system depends on the extent to which there are variable revenues and variable costs. When the amount of variable income is large, and where this income will be allocated is also variable, management discretion is at its greatest. If the amount of variable income is small, even though management has the discretionary power over its allocation, there is not enough money whose distribution is within the control of administrators. Regardless of whether the amount of variable income is large or small, as long as little discretionary power is granted to administrators for its allocation, a simple accounting system is appropriate.

Financial Management and Budgeting

Holosko and Feit (1981) considered that financial management is internal management because it is a question of counting services, the number of service recipients, and the dollars allocated to each unit of service or to each client as well as reporting and types of services and benefits received, and the time and resources allocated to the provision of services.

Financial management supports administrative decisions. It provides administrators with fiscal data to assist them in determining whether programs should be expanded, contracted, or maintained at the existing level. This information enables administrators to determine whether services are properly implemented without runaway costs and whether services are utilized at a level that warrants the current funding. The information supports administrators in evaluating whether goals are attained without straining the organizational budgets. The FMS helps administrators assess what activities, such as service coordination and supervision, are performed by the organization and how much these activities are costing the program. "Financial management, no more or no less than any other management process, is not an ordered process deduced from some normative first principle, but a negotiated reality constructed by the people involved" (Miller 1991, p. 2). "The term 'Financial Management' means different things to different people and in different settings. . . . In the public sector, financial management is seldom a distinct entity. . . . It is divided instead into separate tasks of revenue generation (tax collection), allocation (public budgeting), and expenditure" (Lohmann 1980, p. 5).

Three basic assumptions underlie financial management:

1. Financial management is one of the principal constituents of the management process in human service organizations. The problems of obtaining, allocating, and controlling scarce resources are the sine qua non of human service administration—the crucible in which the success or failure of management is tested. . . .
2. Financial management comprises a set of concerns distinguishable from other managerial issues, such as personnel questions, community relations, and long-range planning. . . .
3. Finally, financial management is considered from an "action" frame of reference. That is, less attention is devoted to the environmental context and structural arrangements of finan-

cial process, and more attention is given to the daily decisions and dilemmas faced by managers. (Lohmann 1980, pp. 7-8)

What Constitutes a Fiscal Subsystem

The interplay among fixed revenues, fixed expenditures, variable revenues, and variable expenditures in a program helps determine the extent of the needed complexity of the fiscal subsystem. The specifications of functions that are required will determine the degree of sophistication. It must be remembered that, as a system becomes more complex, costs will increase (e.g., for specific types of personnel, and the amount of time needed to complete tasks). As the different levels of staff involvement increase, the more political the process is likely to become. Staff will become frustrated and bewildered when administrators insist on their involvement but then see no value placed on their inputs or sense that there is a remote possibility of their suggestions being implemented.

Types of Accounting Systems

Petty Cash Accounting

In petty cash management, staff who are allowed to make use of petty cash should be briefed in terms of the guidelines of its use. The guidelines for cash accounting expenditures are simple and direct—the operation is similar to one's checkbook. The system should record the person, the date, the amount and the (precoded) purpose of its use. Unless there are issues that arise from procurement of this information, no staff involvement is needed.

Simple Bookkeeping

For this method of accounting, forms should be developed for staff members who supply information for input into the FMS at a specific time each month. The information furnished should be reviewed by a bookkeeper. Required staff involvement is minimal unless staff are notified of changes in the reporting system or of changes in what funds are expended for.

Financial Management

Staff involvement would be highest for this form of accounting. However, although there are areas in which staff involvement is necessary, this does not mean that all staff members should be involved. Who should be involved depends upon whether particular staff members' roles and functions involve maintaining the FMS of the organization.

In moving from petty cashbox management to bookkeeping to financial management, we recognize that the degree of human judgment increases.

IDENTIFYING INFORMATION PROVIDERS AND PROSPECTIVE USERS

We have already discussed the importance of identifying the key parties so that their input can be incorporated into the FMS. It is a wise decision to rely on personnel who have service-related types of information. For example, frontline workers and supervisors may know more about the agency's operations. However, administrators may decide that frontline staff members should not be involved in strategic planning for the reason that they may have a vested interest in keeping the operation in its current state.

We propose the following scheme utilizing three dimensions for determining the uses of the types of budgeting and accounting methods discussed previously. These dimensions are: (1) the amount of money involved and (2) whether there are any restrictions on revenues generated or item expenditures. The rationale for considering the first dimension, the amount of money involved, is to help determine whether the effort is worth the staff time and monetary input. The rationale for the second dimension is based on the fact that although some revenues generated have no restrictions regarding the areas in which such monies can be spent, certain other revenues are earmarked for particular purposes. In instances where revenue allocation is predetermined, all that is required of administrators and staff is to monitor activities to ensure that all the monies promised are received and accurately reported in a timely manner, and that monies are spent in the predesignated areas and accurately documented in a timely fashion. In situations where there are significant revenues and latitude in terms of how the money is to be spent, administrators can consult with staff members to determine the areas where the money is to be allocated. The following grid and examples (given for a senior citizen center) provide an illustration of these concepts.

TABLE 3.1

Expenditures	Small Fixed Revenue	Large Fixed Revenue	Small Variable Revenue	Large Variable Revenue
Fixed Expenditure	**Cell 1.1** Petty Cash	**Cell 2.1** Simple Bookkeeping	**Cell 3.1** Simple Bookkeeping	**Cell 4.1** Simple Bookkeeping
Variable Expenditure	**Cell 1.2** Simple Bookkeeping	**Cell 2.2** Financial Management	**Cell 3.2** Simple Bookkeeping	**Cell 4.2** Financial Management

Cell 1.1. For a senior citizen center, a small amount of money is needed for transportation expenses for staff and volunteers. The funds for this purpose can be put aside in a petty cashbox.

Cell 1.2. This may be a scenario in which a particular contribution is made to buy gifts for the patrons of a senior citizen center for special occasions, such as Christmas. Also, it is quite common for center staff to organize a monthly birthday party, for which they would purchase a cake and some refreshments. Expenses of this type can be handled sufficiently with a simple bookkeeping procedure.

Cells 2.1, 3.1, and 4.1. When expenditures are fixed for particular items, accurate bookkeeping with proper documentation is required. For example, it is quite common for different community or business organizations to donate monies for senior citizens for the purpose of organizing a trip or a cruise. In this case, proper documentation would record the names and number of people participating in such an event.

Cell 3.2. For this situation, involving a small amount of revenue, it would not be desirable to utilize staff time and effort in keeping a complicated accounting system.

Cells 2.2 and 4.2. In these two situations, it is anticipated that the FMS can furnish valuable information related to administrative functions such as planning of services; providing more opportunity for staff development; involving staff in nonroutine types of activities so that they get better training and orientation; orchestrating service provision in a more effective manner; making forecasts for future revenues; and keeping good accounting records.

Responsibility Centers and Accounting System

After determining the types of budgetary reports and inquiries that can be drawn from the different scenarios, it is necessary to identify (1) who is responsible for providing information to the FMS, and (2) who has access to information generated by the FMS. The answer to the first question helps administrators to both identify the sources of information and establish responsibility centers, as mentioned in Chapter 2. This is a management issue of information collection, monitoring, and processing. The answer to the second question helps administrators identify the users of these financial inquiries and reports. It also provides guidelines to administrators in determining areas of information overflow and information shortfall.

DIRECT AND INDIRECT COSTS

Differences Between Fiscal Subsystems for Nonprofit and Profit Organizations

What makes a nonprofit agency so different from its business counterpart? Nonprofit organizations often have limitations placed on their funds, they must operate within a fixed budget, they are not able to compete with each other or with a profit company, their surplus funds are to be used to meet the purposes of the agencies, and so forth. Comparisons between the proposed budget categories and the actual expenditures in each category is expected. A transfer of funds from a personnel category to an operating expense category usually is not possible. Use of unexpended personnel funds may be allowed for the purchase of certain items, such as equipment, and on a one-time basis. As Bryce (1978) notes:

[T]he nonprofit budget is a sum of restricted and unrestricted amounts. Budgets in nonprofit organizations should distinguish between restricted and unrestricted sources and uses of funds and show any anticipated transfer from one to another. . . . These funds must be used for the purpose for which they were received. To use them otherwise is to violate the contract under which the funds were obtained. Therefore, it is imperative that when the amount of restricted funds are shown as receipts in the budget it is similarly shown that they are restricted, that is, their plan use is pre-determined. (p. 454)

As previously indicated, social service agencies normally have multiple programs. These programs may have different goals and objectives, which impact heavily on financial management. Funds are allocated to the parent agency for a certain program to be provided. Two or more programs can complicate the financial picture, made even more difficult should the funding cycles be different. For example, funding for a staff position may be apportioned among the multiple programs. Any change in actual funds being allocated, or a disruption in the continuity of a grant/contract, may have serious consequences for the budgeting process—further complicated because a nonprofit administrator cannot simply transfer funds from one grant to another or from one category to another.

Methods of Computing Indirect Costs

One method of allocating indirect cost is the simplified method. It is applicable when every responsibility center or program contributes roughly the same to the overhead costs or according to one simple index. The overhead or indirect cost is divided up evenly. . . . For accounting and tracking purposes, overhead or indirect costs are usually stated as a percentage of direct labor costs or a percentage of total direct costs (labor, materials and other costs directly and exclusively caused by an activity). These percentages are referred to as overhead costs. (Bryce 1978, p. 462)

A second method, known as the multiple allocation method, is applicable when there are different pools of indirect costs (depreciation, personnel, administration, and utility) and the responsibility centers are unequal in their contribution to each cost pool. Thus, the allocation of overhead should accurately reflect the different contributions to each pool from the respective responsibility centers. Under this method, the organization could allocate one set of indirect costs based on direct labor, another set based on materials, and still a third set based on other indices (for example, computer time usage).

> A third type, known as direct allocation, is applicable when the nonprofit organization divides its activities into major responsibility centers, such as fund raising and general administration, and requires each to consider its contribution to overhead as part of its own indirect cost. This method transforms an indirect cost to a direct cost by transforming the activity into an identifiable manageable and controllable responsibility center. . . . The major conceptual task in calculating the overhead rate is the proper classification of costs between direct and indirect. For this reason, an independent judgment, perhaps through an audit, of how the organization classifies costs is necessary before an overhead rate is established. (Bryce 1978, p. 463)

Comparison of Funds Over Time

What needs to be considered is whether there is a rising demand for services. Critics can easily suggest that a rising demand is reflective of nonperformance by these agencies. Where is the justification? Is there a real relationship between the performance of these agencies and the increase in demands for such services? When comparison of program budgets is deemed appropriate, some other factors need to be examined, including the following:

1. Was there a steady increase of staff salary over the period of time? Is staff salary adjusted with the Cost of Living Adjustment (COLA) index or the inflation index, and what increased benefits have been provided to workers?
2. Was there an increase in the workers' caseloads? Are workers spending more time counseling the clients or are they spend-

ing more time in filling out more forms for the different parties?

3. Are workers spending more time with their clients or are they spending more time in case management?

These are some of the questions that can be considered in relation to services. After all, workers in social services are providing services in the same manner as factory workers produce their products. The first question is an economic issue, that is, whether workers in social service agencies are rewarded more than other workers in society at large. The second question involves a political issue: as the demands of public accountability increase, time is spent on this concern. The third question is a social issue: as social problems become more complex and social service agencies become more specialized, service coordination needs increase. This increase demands time. (Chapter 6, on the program evaluation subsystem, will discuss the program effort and program outcomes issues.)

BUDGET DEVELOPMENT STEPS

We are recommending that the following steps be taken in developing a budget. These steps take into account political as well as economic considerations. As stated in the earlier part of this chapter, a different economic-political mix can be anticipated for different types of accounting. While a simple bookkeeping exercise is likely to have a strong economic component and a less-pronounced political aspect, service-related types of financial management are likely to have a strong political component.

Step 1: List all the accounts used in the organization.

Step 2: Classify these accounts as restricted or unrestricted.

Note that the financial implications of Steps 1 and 2 are that there is a need to distinguish whether there is any transfer of funds between restricted and unrestricted accounts, and if so, whether such a transfer is legitimate or not.

Step 3: Distinguish the types of information that need to be kept or archived, and the types of information that need to be updated.

Step 4: For information that needs to be archived, distinguish and label the location and methods of storage for such information. For information that needs to be updated, determine (1) who is responsible for the updating; (2) how frequently the updating should occur; (3) how a user knows whether he/she is using updated or outdated information (e.g., what would be the indicators? what is the time of updating?); and (4) if the updating is in monetary terms, whether there is a need to factor in considerations such as inflation.

Step 5: Agencies should make a distinction among the types of assets (such as interest, dividends, and rental monies) that they receive because some of these monies may have restricted uses while others may not. Determine whether transfer of funds is permissible from a capital budget to an operating budget.

Step 6: Budget development is an exercise in which staff members may have to be involved. Determine who should be involved and to what extent.

Resource allocation affects work, positions, status, and distribution of tangible and intangible goods. It affects staff relations, staff-client matching, staff development, unit growth, and job security and stability. It makes a difference in whether an agency can keep its productive members. At times, we have seen administrators who feel that staff members should not be overtly concerned with budgetary issues since they, the administrators, are responsible for cutting checks for their staff members. This is one perspective.

Step 7: Distinguish the types of costs (fixed/variable costs, common/joint costs).

As mentioned in Chapter 1, more social service agencies are becoming multiservice organizations. Some agencies, such as those which are more established, command greater attention from funding sources; these agencies have other advantages, such as shared expenses which cut down overhead costs. Their employment of personnel with multiple talents also provides an edge over their smaller counterparts, as service coordination among staff within the same organization is both cheaper and more efficient.

Two points need to be raised here. There is a tendency for social service agencies to have multiple interdependent units under the same auspices. This arrangement affects goal-attainment activities.

After all, the goals of a unit may not necessarily be complementary to the goals of its parent organization. The second point is that there will be joint expenses as operations such as accounting, bookkeeping, and stationery and furniture acquisition may be more efficiently provided for if they are centralized. The first point directly affects program evaluation. The second point affects the way joint costs are to be computed.

Step 8: Determine the method of assigning costs to the programs, especially if these programs share similar overhead costs.

Step 9: Compute joint costs to be absorbed by the program. Together with the fixed and variable costs, the total costs can be computed.

Step 10: Determine the units of services. This sounds easier than it actually is. In Chapter 2, we discussed three concepts which appear to be simple, but which may be difficult to obtain consensus for. The first concept is the number of services provided, the second is a headcount of clients, and the third is the concept of beneficiaries. Different definitions result in different counts of units and headcounts.

Step 11: Compute unit costs. This is a simple division of the total costs of the program by the number of units, whether such units are a count of the number of services provided, the number of clients in the caseload, or the number of beneficiaries who directly or indirectly obtain services from the program.

Step 12: Determine who should receive such information and how such information should be used. Determination of the person(s) or unit(s) that should make use of such information is more a political than a rational decision. Even though there are political considerations, a rational basis should be formulated, discussed, and negotiated with the significant parties. Determination of the ways in which information should be used is important. Time and time again, numbers are brought up for discussion. Computation of such numbers is never discussed. The assumptions underlying such computations are never explored. The accuracy of using such assumptions over the years is never assessed, but it should be.

The assumptions underlying such computations should be reviewed and discussed with people who provide the information and people who make use of the information. This review process ensures that all the concerned parties are still aware of the ways reports and charts are produced. The review process also ensures that outdated assumptions could be revised and upgraded accordingly.

Chapter 4

The Service Coordination Subsystem

MANAGEMENT CONTROL THROUGH SERVICE COORDINATION

Financial management deals with resource allocation. In a social service agency, it is primarily a control of the use of facilities and staff time. In other words, it is a control of program effort and program costs. As the market fluctuates between inflation and recession, society goes through periods of free spending and austerity. In times of austerity, social programs are monitored more closely as the cry for public accountability increases. Social agencies are asked to produce report cards on the monies that they receive and the ways in which they spend their monies. Accurate accounting is only one aspect of public demand; the other aspect is whether services provided by these agencies are worthwhile. Thus, the public focus is on both expenditures and services. Administrators, being held responsible for all aspects of agency operations, need to provide concrete reports in these aforementioned two areas to the concerned parties, including the board of directors, funding sources (including private donors), and society at large. It is time for administrators to review the scope of management control.

SCOPE OF MANAGEMENT CONTROL

The three areas of management control are: performance, costs, and results; managers are held accountable in all of these areas (Organization For Economic Cooperation and Development 1982, p. 48). This chapter will examine: performance indicators used in social services; program costs, and the seldom-discussed costs of nonintervention; and whether the successful delivery of services can be considered as a sufficient way to measure program results.

PERFORMANCE IN SERVICE DELIVERY

To assess service delivery performance, it is necessary to determine the number of clients who receive services on a timely basis. Accountability based on expenditure is a form of management control. Documentation needs to be provided on where money is spent, when it is spent, and whether it is spent legitimately according to how it was earmarked.

In a social service agency, the product is the provision of services to clients. There is good reason for us to count heads, whether it is based on individuals, units of services, or number of households. It is necessary to use the smallest unit to capture service information because it is easy to add to aggregate data for future use but it is impossible to break down aggregate data into smaller units of analysis. If we can examine the number of service units, the number of households or the number of clients and compare those numbers with expenditures, we can identify costs.

Task Assignments and Staff Training

Task assignment is one form of resource allocation. An administrator's ability to assign the right tasks to the right persons saves money. Another consideration is the appropriateness of time allocated by staff in accomplishment of tasks. Since time is money, administrators are allocating the agency's resources to that particular area. Assigning tasks and resources to particular individuals is not just a money or a time issue; it is also a process whereby administrators may orient staff to the operations of the organization or build teams with new and old members so that a harmonious environment can be attained. In so doing, task assignments entail more than capacity and monetary considerations.

Staff training is also an important administrative function for a social service agency. Competent and experienced staff members take less time and effort to perform tasks for which they are well suited. Furthermore, there is less liability involved for the organization. Also, without such training, the organization's growth is deterred.

Any profession with an emphasis on "internship" requires the investment of staff training time to enable workers to deal with more complex assignments. The training of social work students, with proper supervision, requires 450 placement hours. Therefore, administrators who are concerned about the economy of services must take staff development and organizational growth into consideration.

COSTS OF SERVICE COORDINATION

Measurement of Performance

In a social service agency, performance is related to the types of services provided, the types of clients served, and the types of benefits received.

An administrator's concerns with performance indicators include choosing numbers that are relevant to the measurement of performance and doing a proper count. Since social service agencies are in the business of providing services to clients, it is logical to examine workers' performance based on the ways cases are handled.

Performance implies task accomplishment, which is contingent upon whether tasks are assigned properly. Administrators should assess the appropriateness of task assignments, including whether innovative tasks are given to workers to enhance their career and personal growth. Job training is an important aspect in the growth of social work professionals.

What an FMS Supports

Holosko and Feit (1981) considered that financial management involves internal management because it concerns: (1) counting of (a) units of services, (b) the number of service recipients, and (c) the dollars that are spent on each unit of service or on each client; and (2) reporting of (a) the types of services and benefits received by clients, (b) the time and money spent on provision of such services, and (c) how, when, and where resources are allocated. The three performance indicators used here are: amount of money spent, services offered, and services received.

Costs of Services and Performance

Costs of services have direct implications for services: they tell administrators the areas in which resources are being spent, and provide warnings about areas in which expenditures are to be closely monitored or curtailed. In a social service agency, a high percentage of its budget is allocated to staff salaries. After all, a program that relies on talk therapy must allocate enough resources to ensure adequate human interaction. A process involving worker/client interaction requires "people inputs." Concerns in allocation of people effort are whether staff members are qualified and whether they get the appropriate training for their jobs.

Does the government provide the organization with the money that guarantees performance results? Many of the community-based social service programs are given the amount of money that enables them to hire one or two social workers and many nondegreed workers.

There are two issues that concern degreed/nondegreed status. The first is licensing, since certificate examinations are given only to degreed workers. Licensing establishes a professional standard and indicates that a degreed worker has the skills and aptitude to work independently. The second issue is that there are almost always two career tracks in a social service agency (for degreed and nondegreed workers). Based on this differentiation, different types of resources are allocated to different groups of workers. In a social service agency composed of professional staff members, paraprofessional staff members, support staff, volunteers, and consultants, management control does not appear to be easy. On one hand, the ability to avert scandalous situations is a big mission for administrators, and on the other, the promotion of self-reliance among trained staff is one way of avoiding pampering and of permitting professional growth. Training, however, costs. One type of cost is organizational liability. At the time that workers learn skills, agencies bear the liabilities. Supervision provided by the organization needs to be sufficient to shoulder this responsibility.

Many professional workers share supervisory responsibilities with the support staff. For example, an agency with volunteers and outreach workers may have a small pool of workers training and providing orientation to a large pool of supporting staff and volunteers. One dilemma is that there may not be a clear chain of command, which may be hazardous to the organization. In the absence of a clear chain of command, crisis is often not met with a unified approach.

If the lack of supervision is a form of organizational liability, it is necessary to examine issues of supervising volunteers, and the changing forms of supervision at times of staff turnover. Authority to supervise must be complemented with the authority to exercise sanctions at times of noncompliance. This is an issue which is easier to discuss than to implement. For example, workers who provide home care to the elderly may seldom see their agency's office-based supervisors, to whom they report. There are quite a few gray areas in which it is questionable whether the provision of help is within the domain of home care providers. Moving heavy furniture is not a job that these workers should perform. However, on-the-job situations may cause questions to arise, such as what size and weight limitations for furniture should be observed by these workers, or what a worker should do if an elderly client insists upon moving a piece of furniture which is larger than what the worker is authorized to assist with. This is a dilemma where operational rules, established with a clear understanding of safeguarding against organizational liability, may become compromised by human judgment. It creates a dilemma for a home care provider if the time of decision comes when outside consultation may not be possible. Organizations dealing with clients whose conditions change rapidly should take special precautions in staff orientation and staff supervision on a periodic and ongoing basis. Service coordination can only be enhanced if new demands can be met by new services. Service providers must also be aware, when there are new service demands, whether their organization can meet such demands and, if not, who will bear such responsibility. Social workers and social service administrators do not dictate the structure of social service programs. The structure is usually prescribed, with little leeway, by the funding sources. Programs that rely primarily on public monies must find other revenues to create a workforce with a proper supervisory structure installed; they must also find revenues to provide the necessary financial incentives. This is a dilemma between management control and financial management.

Implementation of Service Coordination: Case Management

Holosko and Feit (1981) pointed out that administrators should incorporate case information into the FMS. In this respect, administrators can make use of client information or service information in determining needs assessment, service utilization, and client functioning. In this way, Holosko and Feit already established the unit of analysis. In a duplicated service count, they are more interested in the number of clients receiving a particular service. In a nonduplicated service count, they register the number of services utilized by a particular client.

Informational Needs for Service Coordination

The determining factor is how to define a client system. If the client system is defined as families, we may actually be providing multiple services to more than one family member. In that respect, the count of services may be an undercount of the amount of work that workers provide. On the other hand, by counting the number of services, we may have too high a number of services for a selected small number of clients. Who is in the right position to define the client system? This is one question that administrators and service providers should discuss and decide together. After all, statistics that reflect the amount of work and the actual staff effort, measured by hours of work, would assist administrators and service providers in planning of services and preparing meaningful reports to the board of directors.

The three areas of management control that are useful for administrators in service coordination are: workers' performance, costs of services, and benefits of the intervention. Workers' performance is an area in which administrators match the workers best suited to meet the needs of the clients. This is not a question only of competence but also of client-worker styles and previous working relationships. The second area is costs. Administrators cannot afford to have highly trained professionals working on tasks that a paraprofessional or a member of the supporting cast can perform as adequately. (Although cost is an important factor, the intangibles, such as having staff coming together in case conferences as a means of building team spirit and helping members to learn to work in teams, is a facet of service coordination and cannot be overlooked because of the inherent benefits of such an approach despite potentially higher costs.) The third area is the benefits of the intervention. Proper service coordination, by having professional staff meeting to feel involved and to develop a format where staff input on service coordination can be attained, benefits the clients as well as the staff. Better service coordination results in clients not hopping from office to office, and better coordination builds clients' confidence in the services. After examining the three areas of management control (i.e., workers' performance, costs of services, and benefits of the intervention), we ask how this information helps administrators in managing better.

COSTS OF BENEFITS: RESULTS

In human services, results are assessed based on how well people are assisted. Determination is made as to whether client functioning is actually getting better as a result of this process.

When assessing results as a function of client benefits, it is necessary to examine the concept of client benefits. Administrators should determine units of services based on some sort of practice wisdom; units of services should not be based on a concept of convenience. Many of the benefits go to the caregivers who may have to shoulder a great deal of responsibility if public services are not available. Some of the social services benefit not only the clients and their families but also society at large. Let us start by elaborating on the concept of benefits.

Benefits cannot be determined without first identifying who the clients are. The complexity of identifying the clients can be illustrated by several examples.

In a program such as Aid to Families with Dependent Children (AFDC), children are considered to be at the center of the intervention. When a teenager in an AFDC case gives birth to a child, a new case is established under the mother's name. In other words, one case is now turned into two cases. For the workers to provide services to the family, benefits to the child can benefit both cases. In child welfare, workers are assigned to supervise the activities of children placed in the foster care system, and to work with the biological parents in preparation for reuniting them with their children. They have to make contact with the biological parents and with the foster parents who provide the children with a temporary shelter. In elderly services, the worker may provide services to the elderly. Establishment of a caring and trustful relationship with the worker may result in an elderly person's consulting with the worker on some areas of daily living concerns. In the absence of the worker, the *extrakin* may have to provide a more active role in caring for their elderly family member. Job training programs offer classroom or in-service training so that clients can become independent and self-sufficient. In rehabilitation services for mentally handicapped people, services are provided to the service participants and also provide relief to their caregivers. These examples illustrate that it may be easier to identify how many participants there are in a program than to identify who benefits and to what extent.

As the need for services increases, so does the need for service coordination. In social service agencies, we are dealing with a human processing exercise, whether it is maintaining functioning of individuals, the family, or the community. The first type of input in the helping process is the client system, which includes the client and the client's significant systems, that is, the family, the community, the psychosocial functioning of the client, and/or the physical health system. The second type of input is the service provider, which includes the provider's professional training, personal attributes (such as commitment, sympathy, outlook in life), and life experiences. The third type of input is services, whether they are tangible or intangible in nature. The fourth and last type of input is the organization. Information important to management includes the ways cases are handled, the ways workers are organized, and the ways clients are served.

ORGANIZATIONAL ADAPTATION FOR MANAGEMENT CONTROL

Knowing what services are to be provided and the capacity of the staff force, what management control can administrators have?

It has been pointed out by Peter Drucker (1974) that there is no financial incentive for workers in the nonprofit sector to perform more efficiently. Since there is no association between productivity and efficiency, social service agencies have sometimes been criticized for their nonperformance.

How true is it that administrators in social service agencies do not have any control? If the assessment of results is based on rational thinking, administrators can exercise managerial functions such as recruitment, promotion, and demotion. After all, workers are expected to have a proper professional orientation that guides their performance. Their activities are guided by their professional codes of ethics, their professional standards, and the norms and values of the profession. In other words, the form of performance control resembles that of other professionals, such as medical doctors and lawyers. Social workers exercise their professional judgment to guide their activities, with reference to norms and standards written in the codes of ethics of their professional body, the National Association of Social Workers.

Management Control Through Allocation of Rewards

The control of salaries and fringes is a direct form of management control. If administrators have the flexibility to restructure their staff, they can curb expenditures and generate additional revenues. It must be understood that not all contributions can be applied to salary increases and additional fringes. Some agencies also take special precautions in curbing salary and fringes adjustments to keep disputes from arising (i.e., if the adjustments are for selected workers rather than across the board) at a minimum. One way of providing incentives is through a distribution of goods. In social service agencies, a staff member can move up the career ladder through better training and by gaining more experience in working on more complex cases. Some agencies provide "release time" for staff members. Some provide economic incentives through subsidies for workshops or specialized skills training. In comparing staff who receive formal training versus staff who do not, it can be expected that many of the incentives are applied to the first group only. In this situation, alternative incentives should be provided to the second group of staff. Furthermore, agencies which have a small number of professional staff who are charged with the responsibility of supervising a large pool of nondegreed staff members may have a problem in motivating staff members. In some community-based social service programs, the only professionally trained staff member is the administrator who controls the resources. In such a scenario, it is difficult for the administrator to motivate his or her subordinates when the subordinates recognize that there are no career advancement opportunities for them. In this respect, we are talking about curbing expenditures and holding staff accountable for services that they provide. Therefore, service monitoring is one important aspect of the FMS.

Management Control Through Service Monitoring

We mentioned in Chapter 1 that as social problems become more complex, the impact of such problems is felt not only by the individuals but also by their significant partners, their families, and their communities. Furthermore, as the complexity of such problems increases, the number of people in the client system who need assistance is likely to increase. For example, if we examine the lives of welfare mothers, we can no longer talk about a job only. We are going to assess the health, both physical and emotional, of the participants and the children for whom they care and take note of the educational needs of both the mother and her children. We evaluate the family life and the quality of care. We worry about the nutritional value of food and the family cohesiveness if children are brought up in neighborhoods with rundown buildings and an underground economy. If those are legitimate concerns, workers who are assigned to such cases need to provide intervention on many fronts. This means service coordination. This implies that activities must be organized and orchestrated in a fashion that serves these families best. But service coordination is expensive in terms of time. Service coordination is also a political process among the service providers. It may be a war of egos.

Management Control Through Resource Allocation

Administrators may have more control of service coordination among staff of the same organization. After all, there should be an authority structure which allows administrators to direct activities. But coordination with the use of authority may be less welcome than coordination based on needs and commitment.

If service providers are spending more of their time and agency money on service coordination than on provision of services themselves, at least two issues are raised. One is that someone pays. Who is that someone? Can the agency afford this? The second issue is whether there is a more economical way of coordinating without neglecting the needs of the clients or subjecting the clients to the service circus. These issues need to be addressed, whether it is a question of service coordination within the agency or with other agencies. The unit cost analysis will be helpful in this regard.

Control Through Managing Case Activities: Case Flow Management

Case flow information pays special attention to (1) the time when services are requested, referred, and provided, (2) changes in the client systems and the changes in the client-worker relationship, and (3) the difficulties encountered in service delivery. Case flow information is important to middle-line managers in forecasting. In social service agencies, necessary information is furnished by: forecasting the changes in the types of problems presented; the profiles of clients; the service eligibility criteria and their impact on clients; the types of cases that lead to caseload backlog; and the types of client-worker relationships that make a difference in case outcomes.

The concept of case management probably is important for this phase of management. In a business organization, the roles and responsibilities of a middle-line manager are in the area of facilitation. Middle-line managers need to ensure that workers spend their time diligently in production, and that all the tools, resources, and materials required in production are available. In other words, the job includes the avoidance of delay in production. In a social service agency, middle-line managers must ensure that clients who deserve services as a means to combat their problems are provided with such services. Middle-line managers also must ensure that staff who are involved in services are assigned tasks in a fair manner.

Control Through Supervision

Worker accountability is one aspect of management about which frontline supervisors are likely to be concerned. They are probably more interested in ensuring that all the parties are coordinated to a point where service orchestration can take place. This includes a time-table for their supervisees. For example, they are concerned about whether (1) case referrals are responded to; (2) assignments are made so that service accountability is ensured; (3) reports are furnished in a timely fashion; and (4) work is performed according to the guide-lines and rules of the funding sources.

STEPS TOWARD MANAGEMENT CONTROL WITHIN THE SAME ORGANIZATION AND AMONG ORGANIZATIONS

Service coordination within one agency is different from service coordination with other agencies. Internal control is only half of the picture. Service coordination with other agencies without any control subjects the organization to the same types of public scrutiny in the same manner as if the organization were the sole service provider. Some organizations have joint programs with other organizations. For example, clients may receive meals-on-wheels services from one agency and home care services from another agency. Sometimes, nei-ther agency has the sole responsibility in providing services to the clients. Sometimes, one agency has already opened a case with a client, and additional services are sought from another agency for the same client. The first agency does not have control of workers in the second agency, and services obtained from the second agency do not involve contracting out. Staff time, organizational liabilities, authority structure, chain of command, and methods of sanctioning must be addressed in these organizational linkages.

In this section we examine some of the management tools that help administrators monitor staff activities better. The first one deals with internal control; the second deals with intra- and/or inter-organizational linkages. We examine the two areas in which finan-cial management affects the staff: the first one is the types of job assignments and service coordination relating to staff within the same agency; the second area is whether staff is allowed to coordi-nate services with colleagues in other agencies.

Administrators need to establish formal linkages and standards in service coordination with staff outside the organization. They do not have authority over people of other organizations, but they carry liability related to such interagency coordination. Cost analysis of staff activities is useful in assessing the cost of such interagency coordination.

Step 1: Examining the Types of Service Coordination Needed

Administrators can examine the case flow process, identify service gaps, identify areas in which no one in the organization seems to have authority, and examine the costs of service coordination in terms of intraorganizational coordination versus interorganizational coordination. If the costs of interorganizational service coordination are high and the degree of management control is low, administrators must assess whether it is worth such expensive program efforts when organizational liability is equally high. The most economic way is an intraorganizational service coordination with good management control and inexpensive program effort. Unit cost analysis (as mentioned in Chapter 3) provides such a basis in monetary terms.

Step 2: Determining Risks and Effort

Once unit cost analysis is performed, administrators can make use of the following grids to determine whether the efforts, in terms of staff time, money, and facilities used, are worth the liabilities to which the organization is exposed.

TABLE 4.1

Degree of Management Control/Degree of Liability	Management Control (High)	Management Control (Low)
High	Stake - Moderate	Stake (High)
Low	Stake - Low	Stake (Low)

Stake/Unit Cost	High	Moderate	Low
High	Cell 1.1	Cell 2.1	Cell 3.1
Low	Cell 1.2	Cell 2.2	Cell 3.2

Step 3: Administrative Decisions: Effort Worth the Costs

In Cell 1.1, administrators should seriously assess the situation, as both unit costs are high and this form of service coordination subjects the agency to a high-stake situation. Administrators may want to consider whether the agency can incorporate some of the services, currently provided by its partner(s), into its own operation.

In Cell 1.2, administrators must also assess whether the low unit costs are a good reason to put the organization at such high risk. In Cells 2.1 and 3.1, administrators can consider whether better service coordination may lower the unit costs. Case flow analysis and better case management techniques can be explored. In Cells 2.2 and 3.2, administrators can feel comfortable with such situations as it is not too expensive for the organization to provide such services, and the stake for the organization is also moderate or low.

Chapter 5

The Program Planning Subsystem

PURPOSES AND FUNCTIONS
OF PROGRAM PLANNING

When an administrator engages in program planning, he or she is setting goals to direct the future of the agency, based on such factors as projected funding sources and anticipated outlays from such sources; trends in the size and nature of the problems of the client population; and the extent to which revenues are expected to keep pace with expenditures. Goal setting is not a simple task. Some organizations may have difficulty in quantifying their goals; some organizations, having different programs, may have multiple goals which may not be complementary to one another.

Program Planning and Goal Setting

> Goals must not be defined too broadly. . . . Having quantifiable goals is an essential starting point if managers are to measure the results of their organization[s'] activities. . . . Almost any nonprofit organization can establish a benchmark to measure program achievement. (Harvey and Snyder 1987, p. 17)

Social service agencies may have multiple programs, and each program has its own goals and objectives. Frequently, social service organizations are funded by various sources for a variety of services. In addition, one program may have more than one funding source, and different programs within the same agency may have different funding sources. All of this may contribute to programs within the same agency not sharing the same philosophy, goals, or services targeted for the same groups of clients. For example, agencies that are community-based or preventive in nature are likely to offer multiple services as they attempt to meet the needs of clients who may not have jobs; who may have difficulty in gaining access to services; and who are suffering from ailments which have physical, emotional, or social components. These agencies need many specialized programs staffed with trained personnel to handle such complex situations.

GOAL ASSESSMENT AND FORMATION

If done properly, program planning provides direction to an organization, and organizational activities can be designed in a manner in pursuit of the goals of the organization. Some organizations have difficulties in this process. They may not be in a position to formulate a goal that reflects the work of the organization. They may not be able to operationalize the goals of the organization in simple and concrete terms. They also may have goals that are not complementary to one another.

Obsolete Goals

Some service organizations have been established by parent agencies that may have service missions that are obsolete. Job-training programs which are required to place their graduates in jobs have come to a realization that some of the classroom training may not provide the graduates with the skills required in a contemporary labor market. As a result, training will be focused on job-ready clients, who may benefit from such a program. Programs change as opportunities arise as a result of changes in the political economy.

Unexplicit Goals

Some social service programs may have difficulty in stating their goals and missions as they may have difficulty in justifying their services and intended program outcomes. This is especially true when programs are preventive in nature. Programs that are established to reduce the prevalence of a particular social ill may have difficulty in measuring their success in combating social ills. As with a social experiment, how can we establish the cause-effect relationship? How many intervening variables are there? What are our chances of controlling such variables? Would it be ethical to control such variables even if it were feasible to do so?

Moreover, some social service programs are established as a means of social control. The formation of Community Action Agencies in the 1960s is an example. One of the objectives of that program is to help settle some of the migrants from the South; another program objective is the maintenance of social order. Maintaining social harmony among different racial and ethnic groups, integrating "underprivileged clients" into the mainstream of society, and creating social commitment and civil responsibility are some of the major functions of social service programs. Such functions are not always easily identifiable. Thus, sometimes a social service agency has been established to combat a social ill or to tackle a social condition for which society at large had no solution or no understanding of its cause. The exact nature of social intervention is not known even though society has a concern. The goals of such agencies are not explicitly stated. The lack of clarity is very much associated with the nature of the work that these agencies handle. The lack of explicit guidelines may also permit workers to exercise their judgment and common sense.

CAPACITY OF AN FMS
TO SUPPORT PROGRAM PLANNING

In order for an FMS to support the program planning activities of an organization, the designers of the FMS must be concerned with (1) whether the goals of an organization can be operationalized and be measured and (2) how organizational activities can be arranged in a manner to benefit the right groups of clients with respect to the right types of services.

Step 1: Operationalizable Goals

As a first step in goal setting, it is necessary to examine the agency's original mission and the evolving policies that guide and fund agency programs. It also must be determined whether such programs are set up to provide the proper services for the right groups of clients.

When the focus is on the interplay between goal setting and financial management, it is understood that financial management has to relate services to expenditures. If the costs are too high, a particular type of program may not be able to meet its goals. In the same manner as managed care, program administrators dictate the types of services that are more efficient in tackling a particular problem. One strategy is to devise a benefit-and-service equation, with benefits measured by the number of services provided to clients on a timely basis with support from qualified staff. The concept of efficiency can then be operationalized by defining the right types of clients who are likely to be benefited by the least expensive programs.

Step 2: Consensus in Goals and Standards

Goals formed with the endorsement of staff are goals that are likely to be implemented. In brief, successful goal implementation is a process in which staff participation is the key. One of the problems associated with program assessment is the lack of consensus in identifying program goals among the service providers and the evaluators of the programs. Administrators should take a stand to bridge the differences between what evaluators perceive to be staff functions and what staff members perceive to be their functions. How can such a disparity be reduced? Steps should be taken by administrators to involve staff in financial management. For financial management to be operational and effective, one needs to identify the goals of the organization and make the connection between organizational activities and the goals. In that respect, organizational goals must be related to the services offered by the organization. The planning of services should be guided by the future goals of the organization. The evaluation of organizational performance must be assessed against the goals that were set. Unless the components and functions of each of the subsystems and their relationships with one another are defined, management may not be possible.

Step 3: Determining Whether the Organization Has the Staff Quality, the Right Structure, and the Funding to Provide Beneficial Services to Clients

The first question is whether the organization has the capability, namely, qualified staff, to provide the types of services that have impact on the lives of the clients. Frequently, an agency's operation is already established, in which all roles and functions are predetermined. At the time when a contract is funded, the number of positions and the salaries attached to those positions are predetermined. This is somewhat different from a business organization. The creation of a position can be justified as long as the revenue/expenditure balance warrants it.

In some social service organizations, in addition to regular staff, some positions are designated for hiring of clients who are qualified to become service providers: for example, some positions in senior citizen centers are designed for retired employees. In job-training programs such as CETA (Comprehensive Education and Training Act), positions which are created to assist financially needy high school students provide the additional benefits of enhanced life experiences and work experiences for these students. In rehabilitative services for mentally handicapped individuals, employment and training are designed to offer opportunities for individuals to socialize and to feel productive. In cases such as these, the expenditures, namely salaries, serve to hire persons who are also beneficiaries of such programs.

These are some of the intricacies in social services. Furthermore, these are some of the intangible benefits that are real but may make little "economical sense." The point that needs to be made here is that some social service organizations rely totally on contract monies from a single funding source. This is their main, and at times their only, source of revenues. Monies are earmarked for designated accounts on a monthly basis. Most of the expenditures fall into the fixed costs category. In this respect, there are few strategic planning activities that would be impacted by the financial management aspect of the organization. In this sense, the relationship between financial management and strategic planning is weak. For these organizations, a general ledger system which reflects accurately the revenues and expenditures, with receipts and returned checks, may be sufficient. The degree of impact on programmatic operations of financial decisions is low.

Step 4: Goal Setting Is a Process

Sometimes, administrators may have difficulties in setting clearly defined goals. At times, an organization is established to identify community needs and to respond to the needs of the community accordingly. When there are many constituents involved with many agendas, it may not be easy to arrive at any consensus. Therefore, involving different parties in goal setting is a process of negotiation and compromise. Having listed some of the difficulties in goal setting, administrators should examine the tasks that the agency was contracted to perform. There should be some common themes among agencies funded for the same purpose. These common themes would become the common ground for goal setting. The methods of service delivery can vary.

IMPLEMENTATION OF PROGRAM PLANNING

In order to identify the people who should be involved in the financial planning process, it must be determined what kinds of financial decisions affect what kind of management and operations. In brief, there is a need to examine the aspects of the decision-making process of an organization that have budgetary, administrative, and operational implications. In social service organizations, it is necessary to determine what kinds of financial decisions must be made.

Key players in the goal setting process include: the funding sources, as they prescribe requirements through the contracts that the agencies enter into with them; the workforce, whose capacities and expectations impact on goal setting; the board of directors and other people involved in strategic planning, who determine policy and initiatives; and the clients themselves.

Harvey and Snyder (1987) discussed the issue of goal setting in somewhat similar terms.

> How can nonprofit managers deal with the inevitable conflicts and confusion over goals? The answer is not simple, but neither is it difficult to comprehend. Nonprofit managers must work with board members, donors, and other key players to reach an agreement on goals and priorities. . . . must write down these goals and make sure that staff members of all levels of the organization understand and accept them. Finally, they must see

to it that the financial and human resources of the organization are consistently applied to these objectives. (p. 16)

Step 5: Identification of Clientele and the Types of Services That They Received

Some of the key parties that should be involved in the goal-setting process have been identified. Unless the types of contributions that these key actors make are acknowledged, it will not be possible to make a realistic assessment of the work to be performed by the workers in the organizations. An examination of the target population is important because of the changing needs and demands from the community. An example of this lies with the job-training programs in the United States. If the success of a job-training program is measured by the success of placing graduates in real jobs, then we have to examine the skills and readiness of the graduates in landing jobs. Job placement is likely to be more successful with clients who have had basic education and prior work experience before enrolling in the job-training program. Furthermore, clients who can make child care arrangements on their own have fewer worries about finding a nearby day care center which can provide quality care. In other words, the success of the programs lies with the types of clients that are served. Clients lacking both the basic job requirement skills and support from their social networks are unlikely candidates for job referrals or job placement.

OPERATIONALIZATION OF PROGRAM GOALS

Identify Program Planning Areas That Can be Benefited by the FMS

How could the FMS support administrators in program planning? Tyran (1980) stated the following:

Budgeting and forecast plans are used to outline and clarify organizational objectives and programs, coordinate the activities of suborganizations, measure efficiency and performance, simplify management control and assist in financing the business requirements. (p. 28)

Budgeting has developed into an effective and forceful planning tool which is used to establish sound and logical operational and financial control over all aspects of the business activity. It sets forth predetermined objectives and provides a basis for measuring performance against the planned goals. As in the case of any planning performance and making revisions as required to accommodate changing internal and external conditions and new developments . . . It should be noted that the budget plan is more than a series of estimates. It is true that estimates are often used in developing the preliminary budget, but when the plan is finalized and approved, it becomes the basis for the operating and administrative policies and management decisions. The budget plan represents the specification for operating a business. They are not an end in themselves but rather a means to an end. (p. 29)

The following *contributions* from the FMS have been identified as useful for program planning:

1. The FMS sets up a logical sequence among the items that compose such a system;
2. The FMS provides valuable information, some in the form of financial reports, some in the form of case-specific or client-specific inquiries, some in the form of trend analysis, for administrators to support decisions in the areas of budgeting and service planning prospectively;
3. The FMS provides flexibility for administrators to examine service costs, program efforts, and client benefits in units of services or in number of beneficiaries; and
4. The FMS provides information for administrators to examine service utilization patterns, service demands, service gaps, service costs, and trends of funding.

Informational Needs of Program Planning
in Building an FMS

If the information generated by the FMS is to assist administrators in providing direction and guidance to their staff members, a relationship between program goals and program activities must be established.

GOAL SETTING
TO PERFORMANCE STANDARDS SETTING

It is not necessary to succeed in all, or even any, of the foregoing recommendations to make your organization better. Just the process of defining and quantifying goals is healthy. You will be asking the right questions, examining your organization's reasons for being. Even if the best you can do is to agree or disagree on fundamental points, you will at least have addressed them. This self-examination is bound to be better than letting your organization drift, caught up in a swirl of donor-driven projects, procedural meetings, and other mighty distractions that invariably attend a serious charitable activity. (Harvey and Snyder 1987, p. 18)

Case-Related Information

We stated that some program goals and objectives cannot be defined as clearly and explicitly as we would like. The difficulty should not translate into an unguided operation. After all, social workers who are recruited into a social service program usually know whether they are dealing with cases, groups, or some forms of mass programs. They are aware of the reputation of some social service agencies in terms of types of in-service staff training provided; they must have some idea of the types of clients that the agency handles. In other words, even though no two cases are exactly alike, the types of activities performed by the workers could likely be classified as "assessment of client system"; "determination of needs"; "establishment of service contract"; "engagement of clients in an examination of and an evaluation of the client system"; "provision of information and referral of services"; and "preparation of case termination."

Along with the types of activities that can be expected from a client-worker interaction, there are certain behaviors that can be expected from the workers and from the clients. On the part of the workers, it can be anticipated that they would discuss with the clients the objective of the intervention (workers engage clients in discussing their problems and formulating and reviewing service plans). On the part of the clients, certain behaviors can be expected (for example, clients in substance abuse treatment are expected to be free from the influence of drugs from the date of treatment to six months after the completion of the treatment, and are expected to continue to communicate with other family members during the therapy sessions and for a period of six months after the completion of the therapy sessions).

Group-Related Information

Based on the activities and the types of client/worker behavior, it is possible to determine what workers normally do in order to help a particular group of clients. This type of determination formulates baseline measurements of a social work intervention.

STEPS TOWARD CORRECTIVE ACTIONS IN PROGRAM PLANNING

After receiving information from an FMS, administrators can make better decisions relating to program planning in the following areas.

Step 1: Prioritization of Organizational Functions and Activities

Agency administrators, together with the social work profession-als, should establish a list of objectives, functions, and tasks that are considered appropriate for their agency. Workers should also indi-cate the tasks that they need to perform in order to fulfill their professional goals and their individual needs. A relationship should be established between these two sets of functions and tasks. Rod-gers (1993) established a system in which he designed a chart to set up individual tasks. Individual performance was assessed based on the attainment of individual goals and tasks. Individuals were selected by the ranking and rating committee, which rated and evaluated the individuals' performance. The rating assigned to an individual worker affected the annual merit increase. This division of the pie provided a way to ensure that individual performance was assessed by a staff committee and that the rating was tied to a merit system.

This exercise serves two important functions in management. The first function is the engagement of workers in the decision-making process in (1) the evaluation of staff performance by peers and (2) the evaluation of staff performance along with the evaluation of the units or agency. The second function relates a staff performance system to a staff appraisal system. This function is the heart of financial management. In a business organization, the staff appraisal system may be indicated by the revenues brought in by staff members. In a social service organization, staff performance is not reflected by the number of cases that are handled or the number of hours spent with clients. Merit is recognized only when the work of the staff is associated with the improvement of individual/family/community functioning.

Step 2: Setting an Agenda in Which Workers Can Be Involved

Often, workers in nonprofit organizations do not feel that they need to be involved in budgetary issues, while some administrators find themselves bombarded with financial numbers for which they have little understanding. In short, people are not too enthusiastic about being involved in the financial planning process. Why should this be the case? After all, financial management is the management of resource allocation, which is a source of power. In order to obtain a better understanding of this lack of interest by members in nonprofit organizations, it is necessary to examine some of the historical developments of social service agencies.

Step 3: Setting Goals with a Focus on Financial Terms

Social service programs with multiple contracts and a common administrative body may have greater latitude in making financial decisions; furthermore, some of these organizations share a common financial office. The shared responsibility provides an organization with greater flexibility. The shared office also translates into greater latitude in resource allocation. Resource allocation is a political process.

Since services, staff time, and other types of resources are important considerations in program planning, it must be determined whether what services to provide can be dictated; whether it is possible to stop providing services to clients who are unlikely to benefit from the program; whether the funding sources allow gradual adaptation to new challenges; whether these agencies have their own resources that permit them to make changes accordingly; and whether, in the absence of the previously mentioned resources, these agencies are stymied in their efforts to make changes, whether the request for changes originates with the funding source or with the community.

It must be remembered that services are dictated by the policies at the national level. Many of these programs were established as a result of a series of White House conferences with participation from experts and concerned citizens. One example is in the field of aging. The First White House Conference on Aging was conducted in 1970. Major policies for the elderly were enacted into law in 1965 with the passing of the Older American Act, Medicare, and Medicaid. Undoubtedly, some of these programs are implemented at the state level or even at the municipal level because such a service format facilitates greater participation from the local people. Once the format is set, the administrators follow the directives. Normally, an appeals process is in place to ensure that those who are entitled to services receive them. In brief, service eligibility criteria are predetermined by policies established in Washington. Two points merit discussion.

When administrators have little flexibility, they can do little to the product of the organization, that is, services—whether they consider such services to be profitable or unprofitable, underutilized or overutilized, effective or ineffective in combating social ills, and welcome or unwelcome by their staff.

Since the direction of social programs is not established by service providers or clients, it is necessary to map out how financial management can impact on services. The following four steps provide a framework for administrators to carry out a program/service planning exercise, and to benefit from information obtained from an FMS:

1. Identify the users. List the major constituencies that may be affected by financial planning. Ensure that all important members in the organization are included in the financial planning process. Often, financial control is administered by a financial manager, with a financial plan signed by the executive director and by several designated board members, and presented at the annual board of directors meeting. In other words, apart from these few persons, the majority of members of the organization may have no say whatsoever about the budget plan, and this needs to be remedied.
2. Identify the organizational objectives and programs.
3. Examine the operations, the ways services are provided and coordinated, the methods of prioritizing services, and the methods of supervision.
4. Determine the performance indicators used.

Precautions

Program planning is a process. Precautions should be taken in identifying the users of the FMS. It has been pointed out by Tyran (1980) that this is the political aspect of financial management. Since financial management deals with resource allocation, the distribution of goods and services, and rewarding of staff work, it is, in this respect, political. The process itself is a battle among interested parties. As mentioned in Chapter 2, in examining the framework of the FMS, nobody wants to be left out of the process of deciding where goods go. The inclusion of everyone is expensive; the exclusion of anyone can be equally expensive. Where should the line be drawn?

Standardization of goals is not always easy to perform. Precautions should also be taken in establishing organizational goals and objectives. The common dilemma is who is in a position to say which goals should be honored. After all, in a politically volatile environment, few programs can survive without ripples. We mentioned in Chapter 1 that some social service programs have set up objectives that are so global that they reflect little of the program activities. Needless to say, many of the service providers have no awareness of the program goals and objectives. Some objectives have been inherited from the founders without modifications, even though the problems to be handled at program inception are different from those to be dealt with now. Furthermore, many of these objectives are written in a language that makes any service look sensible. Programs are in no form to be held accountable for the attainment of such program goals. Therefore, one way to minimize this confusion is for administrators to organize program activities in a way that allows for worker accountability.

Standardization of performance is equally difficult. The choice of performance indicators is another area in which administrators should take special precautions. It is unfortunate that social service programs are sometimes considered to be the sole service providers while entitlement programs such as Medicaid, Medicare, and Social Security, though called programs, are really administrative bodies set up to administer funds. Whether social ills such as poverty or unemployment can be alleviated depends on more than an appropriate or inappropriate handling of funds. Two issues require a cautious approach. The first is that performance indicators should be selected based on the actual work of the social service agencies rather than the fictional work presumed by service providers. The second issue is that performance indicators, although they should reflect client benefits, must apply only to situations in which both clients and workers can have control. It is somewhat difficult to hold agency administrators accountable for situations in which neither workers nor clients have control. Employment is an example. At times of a recession or a depression, agency administrators can run a perfect program and yet clients' chances of obtaining gainful placement are drastically reduced.

Too much control stalemates staff development. Lastly, caution should be taken in the area of management control. It is not a question of how much control administrators can exercise, but rather how much control administrators should exercise. Overmanagement deters professional growth, which eventually may have repercussions for the organization.

Chapter 6

The Program Evaluation Subsystem

PURPOSES AND FUNCTIONS OF PROGRAM EVALUATION

One of the major concerns in service performance evaluation is whether the chosen indicators are indeed measurements of performance. What is required of workers to report may be, at best, not fully reflective of their actual work and, at worst, may be misleading.

Herzlinger and Krasker (1987) suggested that nonprofit organizations should be subjected to the same type of public scrutiny as for-profit organizations. They argued that:

> [T]he return-on-investment measure is also an appropriate tool to measure nonprofit performance from society's perspective. When for-profits earn returns lower than the costs of capital supplied, the organizations ultimately dwindle away and the capital that could have been invested in them goes to activities that earn better returns. If a nonprofit offers the same services as a for-profit, and if the market is competitive, its returns on and costs of invested capital are relevant measures of performance. (p. 96)

Newberry (1995, p. 250) questioned whether a fair dollar value can be assigned to nonprofit services.

Harvey and Snyder (1987) identified the difficulty of gauging performance with organizations that provide intangible services. "Gauging performance is more difficult for organizations with intangible objectives. The primary mission of a church, for instance, is spiritual—which is nearly impossible to measure" (p. 18).

Before a program can be evaluated, it needs to be understood in its proper context, by examining the following areas: (1) the reasons for which the program was funded; (2) the tasks the program was designed to accomplish; and (3) the measurement criteria of program success.

Reasons for Program Establishment

In Chapter 1, we discussed the nature of work performed by a social service agency. Often, social service agencies have been formed as society's response to new social conditions or new social phenomena. Agencies, having been funded for such missions, may not have the art or the knowledge to combat such conditions or phenomena. Programs should be evaluated in the proper context. In so doing, the evaluators should gain an understanding of the reasons why such programs were funded and the ways in which services are rendered.

Tasks to Be Accomplished

With respect to social service organizations, there are a few issues that need to be addressed before grouping all social programs together under the same umbrella. What is the purpose of the social service program? Can it survive public scrutiny if it performs the job for which it was established? Who decides whether such a program should continue? The first question has to do with the issue of public good, the second involves marketing, and the third concerns organizational adaptability to environmental changes.

Program evaluation serves multiple purposes. One purpose is to evaluate programs in their proper contexts, and another is to provide guidance and direction to administrators and service providers so that the program can be constantly revised to meet the changing needs of the clients and the ever-changing social conditions.

Are these programs properly set up to provide the proper services for the right groups of clients? Unless there is clear definition of the policies that an agency is trying to address, too many assumptions may be made about what a social service program should be capable of accomplishing. Changes in public policy are indeed of interest to administrators of social service agencies. However, as social conditions change, for good or for bad, administrators may not have the funds, the staff power, or even the authority to make changes in the organization to combat such challenges. An example of this is job-training programs. Such programs are responsible for the training of their clients; the success of the graduates in finding jobs depends, however, to a great extent, on the abundance of jobs in the market, especially those which match the skills of the graduates. Simply stated, the performance of a social service agency and the effectiveness of social policies must be viewed in the proper context.

Using the example of job-training programs, the purpose of job-training programs is to train enrollees to have the basic skills and the proper social skills when they go for an interview. Whether the programs are established for classroom basic skills training or on-the-job training depends on the intent of the policy that provides funds for the programs. To understand the nature of the work of social service agencies and the purposes that they serve, it is necessary to examine the policies that have been instituted over the years which guide and fund these programs. Often, social programs are funded to combat a social condition or a social phenomenon, in an area in which businesspeople do not venture. This is not to say that it is an unexplored business area. Often, we are seeing conditions in human functioning which are part of the market economy failure. The Social Security Act of 1935 was enacted as a result of market failure when hardworking individuals fell through the cracks of the social fabric. Stated differently, the purpose of these programs is to provide services to people in their communities in an effort to alleviate some of their pain and despair and to restore some of their daily normal functioning whether on the individual, family, or community level. In this respect, we must examine what services these programs are providing. The concept of public good must be considered since the general public, as well as the service recipients, are the beneficiaries of such services.

If social services are treated in the same manner as other public organizations such as public libraries, recipients include all people in the community. If such services are not to be treated in the same manner as other public goods, the concept of service recipients is more associated with consumers. Depending on the ways services are defined and "recipients" counted, programs may be assessed with different lenses. Musgrave (1985) stated: "The core of fiscal theory addresses the question of what public services should be provided by the public sector, and how much" (p. 2).

Program Success Measurement

There is little debate that program evaluation helps administrators to review some of the program activities or to make appropriate modifications on the service delivery model. The real challenge is to select the right criteria to be measured in a cost-benefit equation, which relates services to expenditures.

In business organizations, a higher number of transactions is equated with greater profitability. This approach does not work well with social service agencies. More clients, more problems, and more services may not amount to anything significant for the resolution of such problems. One area which social workers complain most about is program monitoring. Social workers who take the time to examine the real issues and the functioning aspects of individuals, families, and communities may not be recognized in the same manner as those who make limited assessments and rapid referrals and who do their paperwork more quickly.

MEASUREMENT ISSUES FOR PROGRAM SUCCESS

Measurement of Costs

From within an organization, a program can be evaluated from a standpoint of fiscal accountability by examining where the monies are spent and whether the monies are spent wisely. A program can be evaluated based on service accountability by examining who has been receiving what types of services. Administratively, a program must be assessed by determining whether the right people have been assigned to provide the proper services, and whether program service procedures are in place. One of the measurement tools is that of cost. The fact that the relationship among services, service goals, services outcomes, benefits, and program inputs may not be easily defined impacts on the measurement of costs. Although overall agency or program spending can be determined, often a cost cannot be assigned to the components that comprise such agency or program spending. Thus, for example, in a preventive program where a worker spends several hours counseling a client and the client's family as part of an overall effort to keep the family intact, these counseling sessions may not be aimed at dealing with a particular problem or issue. These sessions may be rare occasions in which family members can share their feelings. The exact value of the benefits of such counseling services and their cost may be difficult to compute. Some of these benefits extend to more than one individual, and it may be somewhat difficult to predict or pinpoint how effective they are at restoring troubled relationships. The murkiness of these relationships creates a real challenge for interpretation in financial management.

If the murkiness of the operation is a real challenge, it becomes necessary to look beyond the service boundary of the organization. Some programs, in order to be effective, need to collaborate with other programs. Some programs need support from different constituents in the community. The importance of maintaining good relationships with other programs or other constituencies is a given, but placing a price on such networking is not. The changing of the problems, of the clients, of the clients' relationships with their families, and of their interactions with society at large are anything but clear or predictable. Therefore, there is a reason to examine the community at large and the world of the clients in a proper context.

Measurement of Client Benefits

Cost justification deals not only with whether money spent can be accounted for, but also with whether money is spent in the right area and for the right purpose. Thus, a second measurement tool in program evaluation is client benefits.

The first focus of inquiry must be on who is meant to be benefited by particular programs, bearing in mind that some programs have a broader focus than others. Programs such as nutrition programs for children, Medicare, and Social Security retirement benefits are set up to benefit society at large. Alternately, there are programs that are set up to assist those who need special assistance from the government. When people talk about the social expenditure of the entitlement programs, they criticize the poor management of the welfare programs. The criticism may help program performance if efforts are made (1) to differentiate among the types of programs, such as those which are merely in charge of administrative overseeing, and those which actually work with clients to help improve their different functioning capacities; and (2) to examine the types of benefits which these agencies have contracted to provide, and to whom.

The failure to recognize differences among programs, in terms of who is to be benefited and by what services and strategies, may lead to program evaluation that makes an incorrect association between program outcomes and program performance. The findings of such program evaluation without an assessment of the programmatic issues may leave service providers confused at best. After all, one of the functions of program evaluation is the provision of guidelines and direction to administrators and service providers so that the organization can grow. Since financial management places heavy emphasis on the correspondence between revenues and expenditures, the right expenditures need to be connected to the right programs and to the proper benefits.

Measurement of Performance

After establishing costs and benefits in the program, there is a need to evaluate program effectiveness. Are services offered to the right people at the right time? Are clients overwhelmed with too many services? Are clients denied services because an agency is not as responsive to clients' needs as it should be? In this respect, worker performance is examined based on (1) worker assignment, (2) operational guidelines, and (3) the workers' rights to intervene.

Should program performance be restricted to the services that the organization was established to perform? We feel that the success of a program must be assessed by taking into account (1) the operations that it is designed for, (2) the ability of staff to perform related tasks in operations, and (3) the degree of autonomy conferred on administrators. Peter Drucker (1974) wrote an article explaining the reasons behind nonperformance of human service organizations. One reason he cited was that the performance of human service organizations is not associated with an economic or monetary incentive. Human service organizations do not make any profit nor do they secure more economic gains if they are successful in their operations.

Measurement of the Operational Guidelines

Before there can be an evaluation of whether operational guidelines are being followed (and if not, how this impacts on expenditures), it must be determined whether the operational goals of an organization are clearly defined. Is there a set of rules or regulations which staff members can follow?

The success of an operation in a human service organization may be not only difficult to define, but may be somewhat surprising to an outsider. Etzioni (1975) highlighted the following as some of the features and characteristics of goals of human service programs: preventive services are not only difficult to define, but the success of preventive services may translate into a light caseload for the workers; some programs are designed to assist a certain group of clients; and the methods of service delivery vary from time to time and from client to client, and therefore, there may not be a set of guidelines consistently adhered to by all agency workers or appropriate for all client situations.

Numerous examples can also be extracted from cases in child welfare services. Society entrusts administrators of child welfare programs with protecting the young members of the society. Society empowers program administrators with the right to intervene on its behalf, with interventions which include involuntary placement, voluntary placement, and adoption. Society has also made provisions for administrators to extend the intervention network to contracted service providers, which are privately owned agencies that have both the interest and expertise to provide similar services. Society legitimizes these child welfare service operations even though the operational guidelines of the private contract agency may vary from that of the parent organization, and at times, the guidelines may be nebulous or inapposite in particular instances within the parent organization or the private contract agency.

FACTORS AFFECTING DESIGN AND MEASUREMENT OF PROGRAM SUCCESS AND COSTS

Service Rights

One of the important features of the measurement of a social service operation is the adherence to the principle of clients' right to services; that is, operational guidelines are also important in the area of clients' rights, but they may also pose problems with respect to program evaluation.

The right to intervene is not granted by society without reservations. For example, in a child welfare case, an involuntary placement must be accompanied by a court decision and by worker testimony. The rights of the clients must be reexamined every six months by the court. The social work intervention must include client involvement. If this is the case, can workers be held accountable? The agency can be held accountable for the workers' performance by certification of workers and certification of programs. These certifications serve as prerequisites for reimbursement of services. Penalties in monetary terms are imposed on child welfare programs when negligence or noncompliance is identified.

Society makes enough provisions for program recipients' rights. Furthermore, the laws impose constraints on service providers, to prevent them from exercising too much of their own discretion. The laws, however, do not always keep pace with the changes in programmatic issues, such as information obtained from research studies which may affect program initiatives. Sibling visitation, for example, may become more of an issue when a program may not be designed to reunite siblings once they are placed apart; the program, however, may still be assessed on frequency of sibling visitation.

FMS Support for Administrative Decisions

After evaluating what services are to be provided, to whom and by whom, the FMS can offer information to administrators for better service coordination since the parties involved in service delivery are known. Furthermore, administrators know how much staff time is required in setting up case conferences or providing one-on-one supervision. The costs can be projected or estimated. The intricacies of dealing with human issues such as who is involved in complicated personnel issues and who is not are more challenging for administrators.

Caseload Management

With respect to management of services, the manager often must make predictions about the types of cases and the sizes of the caseloads that may impact on program budgets. The ability to predict the financial burden on the program is an important aspect of financial management; the ability to make an accurate prediction, however, depends on factors that are external to the program itself. One of the factors is the degree of instability in the environment. The explosion of foster care placement because of bad publicity is an example. When a case that is known to a public agency results in a child fatality and the report of such fatality hits the newspaper, there are questions about the judgment exercised by the workers previously involved with the case. This type of questioning may affect the way caseworkers decide when to investigate alleged cases. In a time when the appropriateness of child removal is not a certainty and yet risks remain, caseworkers may decide that it is safer to place the child in foster care. Another factor is changing human needs and changes in the service delivery model. The inability to return children in care to the homes of their biological parents leads policymakers and administrators to consider the possibility of adoption. Often, administrators are not considering any long-term strategic planning; rather they are caught constantly in addressing one crisis after another.

Management of Program Costs

With respect to management of expenditures, how much does the balance sheet tell? Is there any relationship between the balance sheet and agency and program performance? How can the performance of an organization be assessed if the types of activities in which the organization is involved are not examined? Giving a financial statement without any mention of the program activities may undoubtedly lead to an allegation that neither the concept of program effectiveness nor of program efficiency has been considered. Equating the costs, in terms of salaries and their fringes, with the types of services received by the clients, may be flawed because an overly simplistic assumption has been made. The assumption is that social services benefit only individual recipients, when in fact, some services benefit their families as well, as is the case with services for the elderly. In examining the high cost of financing an elderly person to stay in a long-term care facility, it is common to wonder who can pay for that type of service. Some elderly persons pay themselves; some receive financial support from their families and friends.

Home care services to the elderly, who otherwise may resort to entering a long-term care facility, such as a nursing home, provide direct benefits to the elderly person and indirect benefits to family members and relatives, who worry about both the quality of care and the adjustment of the elderly person. Some services are intangible, such as counseling the elderly prior to entering a nursing home or to help them adjust to their lack of resources resulting from spending their life savings, or counseling family members who are experiencing guilt or other difficulties in placing an elderly member into a long-term care facility. Overlooking intangible services does not give workers due merit. It undermines the real work of social workers.

PROGRAM EVALUATION DESIGN

This section concerns program evaluation design that is used in assessing program activities. The choice of program evaluation design is not based on what the evaluators like or favor—the appropriate design should reflect the actual program activities at the current stage of program development. Thus, for example, if an agency is assessed in the area of program efficiency (defined later in this chapter) at an early stage of the agency's development, an appropriate indicator should be chosen because the agency is not up and running long enough to have developed an efficient mode of operation. Similarly, an assessment of the effectiveness of only the tangible services provided by a program shortchanges an agency that provides intangible services such as counseling. With this in mind, we will explore some of the common techniques or indicators used in program evaluation design and, where appropriate, describe their limitations and the particular situations for which they are inapplicable.

PROGRAM DEVELOPMENT AND EVALUATIVE CRITERIA ISSUES

Program Effectiveness

Program effectiveness is one of the most important barometers of program evaluation. It is a measure of the extent to which a program is accomplishing what it is intended to accomplish. In this respect, it measures (1) whether the program is delivering the right types of services to the right people at the right time, and (2) whether the program is performing in accordance with the guidelines under which it was established. We begin by discussing some of the broader considerations in program effectiveness and then narrow the focus to discuss some of the measures of program effectiveness.

Goal Accomplishment

What are the indicators used by evaluators in determining which programs are successful and which ones are not? In profit-making organizations, the volume of transactions, whether as a measure of sales or of number of clients, translates into the success rate. In social service agencies, the number of clients indicates the prevalence of a particular social phenomenon. In for-profit organizations, demand for services can be treated as an indicator of "good" services. After all, in a world of free enterprise, demand generates supply and, in return, yields profits. In nonprofit organizations, the demand-supply equation is not as clear-cut. Furthermore, it is understood that some services are mandated by society. For example, food programs, such as food stamps, soup kitchens, and distribution of dried food, are not only for the poor but also for the marginally poor. We find some working poor in homeless shelters. These shelters are not equipped with staff who can handle the types of problems brought in by the users. Discharged mentally ill patients require the types of care that professionals who have the expertise, time, and resources to handle such problems can provide.

Program Objective Attainment Measurement

Program objective attainment measurement measures the extent to which a program has accomplished its designated mission or tasks. In using this measure, be aware of the fact that accomplishment of the mission or tasks of a program is impacted by the nature of the problems presented (i.e., how intractable or deep-seated are the problems which the program, among its tasks, is supposed to address) and what resources and capabilities clients themselves possess.

In the manufacturing industry, sometimes the quality and the quantity of products are measured, and other times it is the volume of business transactions. On occasion, results are discussed and there is concern about how much profit is generated for the business. If the same principles are applied to a social service agency, the focus is what kind of products are produced by a social service agency. Some agencies provide job-training programs with the intention of helping clients cope better with their lives. The improvement of coping as exhibited by the client's behavior is a product of individual counseling. The improvement of the client's self-esteem is a product of a self-help group. An improvement in the race relations among groups in the community is a product of community organization. If we are talking about changing a client's behavior, we must assess whether we stand a greater chance of success in changing one client's behavior versus another's. If this is the principle of operation, it would not surprise us to find workers in a job-training program having greater success with someone with a high school diploma and work experience than someone who has dropped out of high school. Social workers, however, must also take care of the hard-core cases, whether, for example, it is in the area of physical ailments, mental retardation, substance abuse, or juvenile delinquency. Normally, a program spends more time with individuals who have a low degree of functionality than with those who have more capabilities. Workers need to provide intangibles to the first group while they may need to provide only tangible services to the second group.

In short, the public image of services in demand in a for-profit organization translates into "good and intelligent" strategies; in nonprofit organizations, oversubscribed services often resulting from problems encountered by individuals or families may require a greater than anticipated expenditure of time and effort. An underestimation of time needed translates into a slow-moving caseload. A slow-moving caseload, in conjunction with a constant flow of new cases, translates into bottlenecking of case activities, which is often interpreted by the program auditors as incompetence. Instead of examining the cause of the problems, critics often tarnish the image of nonprofit agencies. Negative image is a form of liability. However, we must ask the bottom-line question: Does it help to blame the service providers for nonperformance when the conditions remain unchanged? Can society still provide the types of services for its vulnerable members with the knowledge that such services may have limited impact on the existing situation? Can anybody help a homeless family with young children in a matter of a fortnight? Can talk therapists be blamed when a family requires food, medical insurance, day care, and a warm room at night where children can stay with their mothers rather than being "bused away" before most Americans are up in the morning?

Program Process

In profit-making organizations, the process is less important than the outcomes. In Japanese firms, for example, the percentage of the budget assigned to "entertainment" fees may be high when compared with that of their American counterparts. The styles may be different but the measurement of success is the same—the amount of revenues generated. In nonprofit organizations, the process is very important. In social work training, teachers in practice classes spend hours examining cases and reviewing situations with students so that the students know how to define problems objectively, how to evaluate the strengths and weaknesses of the client system, how to establish rapport with the clients and the clients' significant others, how to engage the clients and their significant others in the helping process, how to engage clients in self-introspective exercises, how to examine the social forces that are at play in the lives of the clients, and how to develop service plans with the clients. The building of the "how-to" knowledge with individuals, families, and communities is the basic training in social work. Why? Because there are situations in everybody's life that are stressful, depressing, and emotionally draining. Some of these situation are beyond the control of the individuals, regardless of their worldly possessions. Because of the diversity of needs, different types of support, both in quantity and in quality, and individuals' varying capabilities in dealing with the same problem, the process of helping must be tailor-made. Unless social workers are not to be held liable, making use of their professional judgment in the process is important. But has this process been included in the evaluation of the program? How would certification of workers contribute to the efforts made by the workers? In other words, a closer examination of the process of helping and the objective of the program is needed. Frequently, the program objective does not include such efforts in the mission statement.

Program Efforts Measurement

Program efforts measurement examines the amount of time staff spends in providing services, establishing a meaningful client-worker relationship, or reaching out to the significant family members. In examining program efforts, we must make determinations about what types of services are measured (i.e., tangible services only, or tangible and intangible services) and how the caseload size enters into an evaluation of program efforts.

The choice of whether the program services to be assessed include intangible as well as tangible services affects the determination of program success. One concern is that tangible services are often the only ones measured, or that tangible services are accorded greater weight than intangible services because program evaluators fail to quantify intangible services. The lack of objective measurement is a research issue, but a determination about whether "difficult to measure intangible services" are to be left out is a program evaluation design issue.

While the focus on tangible services for programs concentrating heavily on such services is probably not problematic, a program with a focus on the provision of intangible services would be disadvantaged by a program evaluation limited to tangible services in that an important component of the program would not be assessed. Moreover, such services require more time and skill on the part of workers than services such as information and referral. Another point to be made here is that it would not be fruitful for social work professionals to highlight the importance of intangible services while ignoring the important function of monitoring and evaluating such services or, stated differently, it will not be useful if policymakers equate only the tangible services with program outcomes.

If intangible services are included in any equation, two aspects must be dealt with. The first is the process of setting standards, and the second is the weight that must be assigned to the intangibles for them to be included in the computation. What kind of standards should be used for tangible and for intangible services? Who should assess the performance? Who should be involved in setting program standards? What form of sanctioning would be useful to the clients, to the workers, and to the program administrators?

The difficulties we can anticipate in standardization of the intangibles are the incompatibility of intangible services and standardization (e.g., one unit of child care services offered by an enthusiastic social worker to a receptive family is different from one unit of child care services offered by an authoritarian worker to a reluctant family) and the determination of the significant parties in setting standards.

The incompatibility of standardization is a fact of life in social work practice. The emphasis placed on social work practicum is an indication of learning from the job. Because of the diversity of services, needs, demands, expectations, and circumstantial factors, the art of negotiation and communication is stressed and there may be few guidelines or directions with which to work. Because of such diversities, standardization must be tailor-made. This process should be based on: (1) types of clients served or types of clients that the program is targeted to serve; (2) caseload; (3) length of engagement; and (4) jurisdiction of services.

Shifting the focus to the size of the caseload, we should note that the problem with setting a target caseload number as a measure of program success is that some agencies do not welcome a high caseload. This will include agencies that deal with high-risk, chronically ill, and frail elderly. Why? Home care agencies may not have the medically trained personnel to monitor the health conditions of these elderly. Agency administrators are unsure whether promises that they obtain from family members or friends will be honored all the time, some of the time, or hardly at all. Promises made by a sixty-seven-year-old daughter-in-law may have sounded good three years ago, but she grows old like everybody else. Her own health conditions may prevent her from fulfilling such a promise. Agencies that are involved in job-training programs encounter similar dilemmas. Why? The chance for a graduate in a 1960s job-training program to find a job in the private sector is greater than that for a graduate in the mid-1990s. This is partly due to the changes in the sectors of the economy in which there is a high demand by employers for workers. This is also partly due to the number of full-time, career-oriented jobs created in the private sector. But the success of a process depends on whether the clients are receptive or whether the problems encountered by the clients can be adequately addressed by the program.

Types of Clients and Types of Cases

In social work, a successful intervention may lie with the skills and commitment of the social workers. There may also be an element of luck. Social workers may at times feel blessed because they find joy in helping some individuals/clients who comprehend and appreciate their efforts. Some clients come with a clear set of goals when they approach an agency. Some clients have a greater sense of awareness of their problems and can admit to their own deficiencies. Some clients' problems are not as deep-seated as others. Some problems involve only the person who approaches the agency; others involve many people and many issues. In short, the complexity of the problem, the chronic nature of the social conditions, the multiplicity of issues and parties, the willingness of the clients to accept their own problems, and their expectations of the service encounter are important contributors to the determination of whether there is a successful service encounter. The skills of the worker may be a consideration but they may not be the primary consideration. Therefore, a worker's performance is very much dependent upon the types of services provided, the nature of clients' problems, and the willingness of the concerned parties to engage in a service encounter.

Furthermore, clients are not always easy to convince to participate in the service encounter. Some social services, such as counseling for gay, lesbian, and bisexual youths, carry a certain degree of stigma. Services to the elderly and children have traditionally been better received by society. Other social services that are geared toward the poor and drug addicts do not attract clients. A fair amount of persuasion is required for clients to participate. These services include child welfare services where children are placed in a foster care system and the court is the designated agent to monitor the progress of client functioning and family functioning.

The nature of the cases presented to social service agencies also results in human judgment calls; thus, different workers may respond differently when encountering similar situations and a course of action deemed appropriate in handling a particular case may be inappropriate to handle a second case with a different set of circumstances. A few examples follow. In child welfare services, there was an explosion in caseloads in the mid-1980s. Why? The initial reaction is that there are more families alleged to have incidents of child abuse and neglect. Another explanation is that people are reporting more cases to the authorities as the reporting system improves. A third reason is that workers are more likely to recommend placement without waiting as a result of adverse publicity. Therefore, workers may subscribe to the motto "when in doubt, place." Similarly, a social worker making an assessment of the viability of older people with dementia living alone sometimes makes a judgment that is not free of doubts and uncertainties. One consideration is the availability of a "good" nursing home facility in the neighborhood. Another consideration is the safety of the older person who lives alone. A third consideration is the social detachment experienced by the institutionalized elderly. The last but not the least consideration is the safety of the neighbors of the older person. A decision made by one worker may vary somewhat from that of another based on the four reasons cited previously.

Indicators of a Successful Intervention

Length of engagement of clients. In the social work profession, one of the indicators commonly used in determining a successful case intervention is premature termination of cases. On one hand, we would like clients to continue with services so that they can be helped more extensively. There is, however, no clear indication that the length of the engagement affects the outcome. The length of engagement affects two issues. The first is the number of cases that workers can take on; the second is that the longer a worker stays on a case, the more expensive are the services—this affects financial management because staff time is money.

Utilization of services. Some program evaluators consider service utilization as a measure of program success. This notion assumes that each unit of services carries the same weight as other units of similar services.

Profit-making organizations will design and implement services that maximize their profit returns. Strategic planners may eliminate services with a low return rate. Banks will not provide loans to clients who are not worth the risks entailed. Can social service agencies exclude clients who are too difficult to handle? In child welfare services, service providers must substantiate that clients are at risk of child abuse or neglect before a case can be reimbursed. Agencies dealing with hard-core cases are likely to be ineffective in providing services that will translate into better individual or family functioning. Hard-core clients also tend to receive more services over longer periods of time.

Additionally, changes in caseload size may mean different things. On one hand, it is easy to assume that expansion of caseload size translates into greater demands from the community. On the other hand, it might also be concluded that a shrinkage in caseload size means better prevention, which subsequently leads to fewer demands.

Worker time and effort. The relationship between caseload and workload may be somewhat difficult to establish. The complexity of the cases, the number of problem areas, the number of people involved, the duration of problems, and the existing resources in handling these problems affect the effort that needs to be spent on a case. Since these factors fluctuate over a wide range, the time and effort expended by the worker and the resources needed from the agency vary. Because of such variations, standardization of case activities is hard to achieve. The lack of standardization makes it difficult for program administrators to estimate the time required for the accomplishment of these tasks. This is a challenge to unit analysis.

Program Efficiency

One indicator of program efficiency is a measure of whether services can be provided to the same number of clients at a lower cost or with fewer staff hours. Comparison of costs of different program activities is one way of determining whether some programs are more efficient than others. Frequently, program evaluation is a term that is broadly defined. Sometimes, it refers to the concept of program effectiveness; sometimes, it deals with the concept of program efficiency. At times, it measures program efforts.

Often social workers are frustrated by the mere fact that they are asked to report on a regular basis the number of people who participated in their group; they have never been asked whether participants are enthusiastic about participating. They feel that they are being scrutinized according to two different sets of standards. While administrators ask for the number of participants, supervisors ask them to describe issues related to group acceptance, group cohesiveness, and group development. The different expectations may result from different orientations. Based on their training, workers can sympathize with their clients, and they are more than likely to ally themselves with their supervisors. After all, the questions posed by the supervisors help the workers in the area of professional growth. Inquiries about the number of participants sound superficial at best, and, at worst, bring mistrust. In order to reduce worker misconceptions about administrators, evaluators and administrators should explain to workers what they are trying to evaluate and how they make use of the findings. One of the most important concerns in program evaluation is that the results of such inquiries leads to a better design of services, with more clients receiving services. It provides information for administrators in two areas of management: cost saving and improved services.

Another indicator is program costs justification. Two aspects of financial management can benefit program evaluation. The first is whether costs can be reduced; the second is whether services can be improved. These two issues are highly related. In social service organizations, we talk about types of clients, types of problems, and the appropriate mix of tangible and intangible services. If we neglect the distinction between tangible and intangible services and the costs of such services in program evaluation, we wonder what kind of incentives workers have to reach out to reluctant clients or to engage uncooperative families in self-introspective exercises. Furthermore, if agencies are not given the time or the resources to start off a new program, the well-established agencies stand a better chance of incorporating new programs into their existing structures.

Cost Containment

Cost containment may be difficult because of the decentralized nature of social service programs. Agencies are funded to run different programs with the intention of addressing the various needs of communities. This is a feature of a decentralized social planning model. In a way, it is the direction of the federal government to empower its local constituencies so that they can tailor their programs according to the needs of their localities. Because of this model, the structure of local social service agencies is likely to have the following characteristics: (1) small in size to limit the effects of bureaucracy; (2) staffed with local people so that the values, philosophies, and orientations of the local service providers are similar to those of the community; and (3) services provided in a manner that is appropriate for specific communities. In other words, a lot of leeway is provided for the administrators and service providers. However, the flexibility of service provision is costly. Custom-designed clothes cost more than mass-marketed styles, and the same is true of tailor-made social services.

INFORMATIONAL NEEDS AND TYPES OF INFORMATION GENERATED

Implementation of Program Evaluation

This examines some of the factors necessary to determine what program evaluation strategies are appropriate in assessing program efficiency.

Nature of Agencies and Phases of Development

As previously mentioned, the concept of efficiency is based on program costs, that is, whether certain outcomes or results can be attained with less effort and at a lower cost. Before computing costs, something must be known about the clients and the services. Assessment of program outcomes or results makes sense when sufficient knowledge is gained about the clients, the types of services provided, what works for which group(s) of clients, and why some clients can be assisted and some cannot.

Stage of Program Development

Some indicators may be more appropriate if the focus of the evaluation is on program efforts. Some strategies are more appropriate for established programs with clear operational guidelines than programs that are still in search of a formula for service provision. Even though unit cost analysis can be conducted on services, it is necessary to be careful in the examination and the interpretation of the results. In exploring the trend analysis of unit costs for services at the three phases of program development set forth in Table 6.1, it can be anticipated that the unit cost will decrease as the program progresses. As staff maturity increases and methods of service coordination are consolidated, a lower level of program effort is expected. The lowering of program efforts, as measured by the number of hours spent by staff and the number of hours during which facilities are utilized, translates into a more efficient performance.

Choice of Evaluative Strategies

Table 6.1 provides a framework for program evaluation with an emphasis on cost/service benefits. This table indicates that certain program evaluation measurements can be more appropriately applied to social service programs at different stages of program development. The two cells marked with "[X]" are considered more appropriate measurements. At the initial stage of program development, administrators engage in writing rules and guidelines for the operation, setting up personnel policy guidelines, exploring needs of the community, and consulting service providers in the community over service coordination. At this phase of program evaluation, the costs of services are expected to be high and the actual units of services are likely to be small. In addition, if program effectiveness is a measure of whether clients who need services obtain the right services, then a measurement of this at the initial phase of program

Table 6.1. Stages of Program Development and the Use of Program Evaluation Criteria

Measurement/Stages	Program Effectiveness	Program Efficiency
Initiation	Cell 1.1	Cell 2.1
Implementation	Cell 1.2 [X]	Cell 2.2
Results	Cell 1.3	Cell 2.3 [X]

development may not be appropriate. This measurement works when the program is at the second phase of program development at which point workers are recruited, trained, and oriented to reach out and make contacts with the clients, with other service providers, and with community members.

Information Needs

Table 6.2 and the material that follows sets forth the information components needed at different stages of program development. In Cell 1.2, service-related information is needed because it represents a program that is in its implementation stage, and program effectiveness criteria is being applied in its measurement.

Cell 1.2 is a program that is in its full implementation stage; the criterion used in evaluating the program is program effectiveness, and the types of information needed are likely to fall into one or more of the following categories:

- *Staff:* Staff capabilities; staff qualifications; staff experiences; staff-worker relationship; staff's ability to offer services to clients.
- *Clients:* Family composition of clients; clients' request for services; clients' problems; clients' abilities to help themselves; clients' self-esteem.
- *Services:* Types of services; length of services; clients' involvements and services received over time.

Cell 2.3 is a program that is in its full implementation stage; the criterion used in evaluating the program is program efficiency, and the types of information needed are likely to fall into one or more of the following categories:

- *Staff:* Staff time on case/services; staff qualifications; staff experiences; staff-worker relationship.
- *Clients:* Family composition of clients; clients' request for services; clients' problems; clients' abilities toward self-help; clients' self-esteem.
- *Services:* Types of services; length of services; clients' involvements and services received over time; service unit costs; staff caseload.

Table 6.2. Program Evaluation and Information Needs

Cell Number	Information Needs	Information Sources	Months in Calendar Year	Nature of Information
Cell 1.1				
Cell 1.2				
Cell 1.3				
Cell 2.1				
Cell 2.2				
Cell 2.3				

The scheme in Table 6.2 indicates that the two cells, cell number 1.2 and cell number 2.3, represent a stage in which a program can best be evaluated using either the program effectiveness or program efficiency criteria. The other cells in Table 6.2 represent a mismatch between the stage of development and the appropriate choice of evaluative criteria.

CORRECTIVE ACTIONS BY ADMINISTRATORS

How are administrators to make use of the information generated from program evaluation? The importance of dissemination of program-related information deserves special attention. The explanation and interpretation of the program evaluation exercise is crucial. After all, staff members who give administration carte blanche to examine their cases, talk to the clients, assess their time logs, open their personnel folders, and computerize all their organizational life information into a "system" may like to know what the "system" thinks of them.

At times, social workers complain that they have been asked to furnish numbers and reports to their funding agencies with the knowledge that these numbers are used as a form of program assessment. For example, in a senior citizen center, social workers report the number of people who participate in activities such as physical fitness exercises while social worker interactions with clients go uncounted. The following provides an illustration of the foregoing. Social workers are often stopped by participants in the hallway to answer some questions regarding program eligibility and information. Social workers answer questions when someone calls for an elderly member regarding long-term care services. Unless the workers carry a notebook and check off all the activities they perform, their numbers of phone or face-to-face contacts, which for a lack of a better term can be called "unstructured activities," normally are not reported. Reporting the number of people participating in organized activities such as the physical fitness class may provide good statistics for the Department of Human Resources but such functions as providing information and referrals and relationship counseling may consume more of the skills and time of the social workers. A mismatch between what is being performed and what is being assessed leads to a mistrust of management and a mistrust of the information provided.

Political Aspects of Program Evaluation/ Financial Management

Apart from identifying the types of informational needs, administrators must designate staff members to provide the necessary information for the FMS. There are two aspects to designation of tasks. The first is to identify those who are the information providers, that is, those who are responsible for informational input into the system (not to be confused with data entry). The second aspect is the identification of those who are the informational receivers, that is, those who receive reports and have the authority to gain access to the database.

A mistrust of management means that people do not feel that management can lead, supervise, or direct. In an agency where management requires input from service providers in shaping programs, in deriving standards by which performance can be assessed, and in serving as the bridge between the agency and the prospective clients (and, to a great extent, the communities), such a mistrust jeopardizes the line-staff relationship. In a social service program, the unstructured types of worker-client contacts are much needed and occur frequently in a day. Reporting only the organized case contacts with proper documentation undermines the types of activities provided by social workers in such a setting. The underreporting may lead to an interpretation that services are ineffective and inefficient. When underreporting leads to such an interpretation, social workers may feel uneasy about management. When an organization is in a stable state of affairs, administrators and funders rely on the professional judgment of the workers and place higher values on the unstructured type of client-work contacts. When the organization is under public scrutiny, administrators or funders may use the operations structured organizational activities as a way to measure performance. This creates uneasiness between management and staff.

A mistrust of the information that the workers are asked to furnish is another problem area. Social workers have been asked to provide numbers in which they do not believe on their programs. An example of this is the number of clients participating in one of the programs in a senior citizen center. In some of the mass program activities, who really participates on a regular versus an infrequent basis is open to interpretation.

Computerization of Information Generated by Program Evaluation

We classify financial management into two types: forecasting and control. In Chapter 3, we called forecasting types of information proactive and we considered information used in management control reactive. Such a classification serves two purposes: information storage, that is, the way data files are organized; and the time for which information needs to be archived. With respect to information storage, FMS information is organized in six areas: (1) agency-related types of information; (2) information on staff members; (3) information on clients; (4) information on services; (5) sources and amounts of funds received; and (6) types of expenditures. (For details about the types of information captured in each of the six areas, refer to Chapter 7, which discusses data management.)

Information Technology and Financial Management

This aspect of the FMS deals with how available the information should be. It is helpful to the designers of the program to identify information that may be needed on an ad hoc basis and information that should be generated in report forms. This is a matter of on-line capability. At this point, it may be argued that, as long as there are computers with greater storage capacity, all information can be on-line. In Chapter 7, we discuss that this is not an issue of computer technology. A bigger concern is who in the organization should have access to the information, which is both a political and a system security issue.

Chapter 7

Computerization of the Financial Management System

After identifying the four administrative subsystems that an FMS supports, this chapter aims (1) to organize the information needed by an organization to provide support of those four administrative subsystems, and (2) to identify the types of information, in reports, that the FMS can generate.

In each of the four administrative subsystems, we identified some of the information that can be generated. For example, in program planning, administrators may make use of information captured and processed in the FMS in the analysis of service and expenditure trends. The examination of these trends helps administrators to predict service demands, service utilization, staff time allocations, and budgetary constraints. For service coordination, administrators can identify case-related issues in their organizations. Information may assist administrators in identifying service gaps and services that cost too many staff hours or too many dollars. The information generated by the accounting/budgetary (fiscal) subsystem provides administrators with both service-related and expense-related information, which may be used as a platform with policymakers such as the boards of directors or funders. The program evaluation subsystem assesses the appropriate use of funds or staff time in areas where clients can benefit. The types of information that can be expected from these four subsystems can be organized into hierarchical forms. An examination of the types of information used by the four administrative subsystems, namely, fiscal management, service coordination, program planning, and program evaluation, leads to the conclusion that information can be categorized into six broad areas: services, clients, staff, agency, revenues, and expenditures.

DATA MANAGEMENT

There are six major data management components in this financial management system:

1. Services
2. Clients
3. Staff
4. Agency
5. Revenues
6. Expenditures

In the chapter on fiscal management, the types of fiscal management that the organization needs were assessed. For a simple checks-and-balances system, the use of a spreadsheet such as a Lotus Spreadsheet may be decided upon. Statistical analysis with statistical testing, such as Statistical Package for Social Sciences (SPSS), may be selected if the decision is made to employ a statistical analysis; a database that can be converted into SPSS can be identified. Therefore, the choice of a database is subject to an assessment based on the following criteria: (1) the information-processing capacity of the organization; (2) the amount of money that is available; (3) the types of reports needed by administration; and (4) the types of accounting systems needed.

Readiness of the Organization in Adapting an FMS

With respect to the four administrative subsystems, administrators need to assess whether the FMS should be designed for one or more of fiscal management, service coordination, program planning, or program evaluation. For some organizations, service coordination may be identified as the only administrative subsystem that an FMS needs to support. For some organizations, administrators may want to plan for the future, but an assessment of the staff sentiment reveals that the resistance to change is so intense that any major restructuring of staff activities, such as service coordination, brings adverse effects to the organization.

Application of the FMS Framework to Work Site

Step 1: Identification of Informational Needs

The first step is the identification of informational needs, which is contingent upon (1) the availability of information and (2) the readiness of the organization in having an FMS.

Informational availability. The first aspect of computerization is the determination of who the users of this system are. Once we identify the users, we then ask: What information do they need from this system? Based on the requests, we examine whether such information is readily available.

If it is readily available, we then ask what we need to do with the information. If information required is readily available and we need to do nothing with the information, we have reason to be suspicious. Why are they still making such a request? Who are the holders of such information? Such an inquiry leads to an examination of the decision-making part of the organization, its structure, its power distributions, its staff relations, and its methods of control and coordination.

If the information is not readily available, we have to ask another set of questions. Where is information located? Who has the information? Do administrators have the authority to make demands to obtain the information? Are providers of the information happy with this arrangement? Was there a concern? Was the concern legitimate?

Currency of information. After exploring what is available, we decide what information is needed for what types of reports. The reason reports are classified as proactive or reactive is that these two types of reports are operating under different time frames. If it is a question of analyzing historical data, we can assume that on-line services may not necessarily be needed. If we need current information on a frequent but ad hoc basis, we may be asking for on-line capability.

Step 2: Determination of the Users

The second step is the determination of the people and the units that should be involved, and the extent of their involvement.

What needs to be fed into the system? What are we expecting out of the system? Who is responsible for providing what types of information? Who has access to the systems? There is no formula that administrators can borrow. These questions can be answered only with negotiation, training, orientation, and maybe, some hard bargaining.

Preparation of staff. Preparation of staff is an important component of this computerization process. Whenever information is requested from staff, there is good reason for staff members to wonder what conclusions will be drawn by administration. The mistrust occurs when administrators sell the idea of automation with such enthusiasm to the staff in the beginning phase of the system design and they pay no attention to staff input once the system is fully implemented. Sometimes, staff are encouraged to participate in the beginning phase of a new project as if their participation is the key to successful implementation. However, once the system is in operation, the level of staff involvement falls.

Information and Reports Generated

Step 3: Determination of Informational Dissemination

The third step is the determination of the way information is to be processed and disseminated.

INFORMATION MANAGEMENT

We believe that data collected by social service agencies are often not turned into reports that help administrators in substantiating their work, mapping out strategies for the future, providing a platform for discussion in areas of goal and objective setting, and establishing performance standards for evaluation. All these functions, if done on an ad hoc basis, may prove to be too expensive in the long run. The lack of system maintenance will soon result in outdated reports. Administrators may have difficulty in persuading staff to furnish useful information when staff do not understand the usefulness of reports produced. Producing reports without quality control may result in wasting valuable staff time.

Instead of creating confusion for the staff, administrators need to identify the level of staff involvement and the areas of their involvement (such as information collection, information processing, and information dissemination).

Decision Support for Management

It must be pointed out that information is good only when it is functional. What is particular information good for? Is it good for solving a particular problem or providing better understanding of a particular issue? Is it good for people at the strategic apex or is it good for someone in operations?

Step 4: Determination of the Way Information Is to Be Used

The fourth step is the determination of information flow in the system.
Information inputs. What kind of information is useful for a particular issue? In Chapter 2, we presented a framework of the types of information that benefit both the FMS and other administrative subsystems. This framework provides guidelines to administrators on the ways in which information generated from financial management help support the functions of those four administrative subsystems.

Information Dissemination

Administrators, with support from staff, must control information that goes into the FMS and information to be disseminated to staff members of the organization. Unless there is a fair amount of control, administrators may find that information in the system is dated, obsolete, and unusable. Once that occurs, staff members lose confidence in the system. In contrast, administrators may find the organization flooded with information that is either not used in the manner for which reports are generated, or that reports are misread and misinterpreted in a manner that is damaging to the functioning of the organization. Based on these concerns, we suggest that administrators should examine the types of information that should be made available to staff at different levels of management. Information can be provided either in the form of reports or of inquiry functions. In Table 7.1, we provide a grid in which two dimensions are used. The first dimension is a level of management. Administrators involved in strategic planning in most organizations need information in making forecasts, while middle-line managers need information in ensuring that there are no runaway budgets and that clients will not be lost in the service delivery system, which is a form of internal control and service monitoring. This is reflected in the horizontal axis of Table 7.1.

Table 7.1. Knowledge Needed to Be Generated by the FMS

Purpose/Utilization	Internal Control/Monitoring	Forecasting
Revenues	Cell 1.1	Cell 2.1
Expenditures	Cell 1.2	Cell 2.2
Services	Cell 1.3	Cell 2.3

Information Collection

We divide the types of information into two categories. The first category is for reactive action, and the second is for proactive action. We further divide information generated in the second category into three components: (1) revenues, (2) expenditures, and (3) services. Each one of these three components requires somewhat different information, and the techniques employed are somewhat different. We present the categorization in the form of a grid in Table 7.1, which helps administrators in determining what information to use.

Step 5: Choice of Strategies

The reason we call it a choice of strategies is that the determination of information needs and the dissemination and use of information must be conducted in a manner so that staff members do not feel overlooked, information is not misinterpreted nor distorted, and organizational functioning is not jeopardized.

The fifth step is the choice of strategies for the processing of information. In other words, administrators need to determine what information needs to be collected, stored, processed, and disseminated. Table 7.1 proposes a scheme for examining how information pertaining to revenues, expenditures, and services is used by administrators. Some information is useful in monitoring services and expenditures. Some information is useful in making forecasts and predictions about the ways monies are spent.

The ways information is to be managed depend on (1) the types of information that are to be collected and coded in a computer system, (2) the types of information that need to be stored in computer tables and files, (3) the types of information to be upgraded and the intervals at which information will be upgraded, and (4) the ways information in the computer system is made available to the users.

The types of information in a computerized FMS can be identified by examination of whether the user is dealing with information on monies received by an organization (called revenues) or information on the ways monies are spent (called expenditures). The user wants to know whether an organization allocates staff time and resources to service provision. In Table 7.1, these three categories form the vertical dimension. Another dimension is the time factor, that is, how quickly is information needed by the users. It can be anticipated that some information must be on-line as retrieval of such information may come from different actors and on an ad hoc basis. Some information, such as a monthly or a quarterly report, needs only to be generated on a periodic basis, whether or not the time of production can be planned for and inserted in a report production calendar.

Based on these two dimensions, some of the indicators that can be generated by this computerized FMS supports administrative decisions in the four administrative subsystems. After identifying the indicators that may be used in this computerized FMS, the user can organize the data elements in tables and files according to the nature of information, which can roughly be categorized as revenues, expenditures, and services.

Based on the information needs, administrators can determine with the system designers the individuals or the department units that require financial management information in order to furnish them with better administrative decisions. Some units, such as book-keeping units, require information on the monetary transaction of each department or unit. Information on clients and services may not be important for people in those units. On the other hand, department heads need to know the source of monies, how much more will be coming in before the end of the fiscal year, what monies are expected to be spent, how many staff hours are likely to be spent on a service area, and how many clients are currently receiving services. Table 7.2 provides the administrators with a way to examine the types of information that can support such adminis-trative functions. Identification of information sources is also important because it dictates who and which units should be respon-sible in maintaining and upgrading the information.

Information Usage

Indicators used for each cell in Table 7.1 are as follows:

Indicators for Cell 1.1: Internal Control/Monitoring of Revenues

- a. Monies received
- b. Monies budgeted for this fiscal year
- c. Contributions
- d. Private funds—interest and dividends

Indicators for Cell 1.2: Internal Control/Monitoring of Expenditures

- a. Trend analysis of the degree of "fit" between what is allocated versus what is actually spent for each type of service
- b. Funds committed for this fiscal year
- c. Funds expended
- d. Fixed item expenditures
- e. Variable item expenditures

Indicators for Cell 1.3: Internal Control/Monitoring of Services

- a. Trend analysis of different services
- b. Trend analysis of unit costs

c. Trend analysis of service utilization
d. Trend analysis of service utilization and service costs together
e. The timeliness of services provided
f. The number of services provided
g. The time between case opening and case termination
h. Caseload ratio for workers of the same unit
i. Caseload ratio for workers of different units
j. Reason for case opening and closing
k. Milestone accomplishment in cases over time
l. Appropriate signatures obtained for authorization of services
m. Appropriate referrals are documented

Indicators for Cell 2.1: Forecasting of Revenues

a. Trend analysis of revenues
b. Trend analysis of expenditures
c. Anticipated budgets

Indicators for Cell 2.2: Forecasting of Expenditures

a. Anticipated changes in expenditures due to inflation
b. Anticipated changes due to supply of workers
c. Anticipated changes due to cutbacks in areas of services, research, or others

Indicators for Cell 2.3: Forecasting of Services

a. Changes in types of problems
b. Changes in types of clients approaching the agency
c. Changes in time spent on cases
d. Changes in service criteria
e. Impact of changes in service criteria on clients receiving services
f. Anticipated changes in the client system, such as changes in the family system, the location from which they come, the types of problems presented, and the changes of the community in terms of security, education, health, school, and recreational systems

Step 6: Information Management

The sixth step is the determination of information management.

Organization of information. In Chapter 1, we mentioned that different administrative subsystems are supported by different financial reports. For example, simple bookkeeping probably utilizes something like a general ledger system where information on revenues and expenditures will be set forth. In an FMS, we believe that unit cost analysis, which utilizes information from both the service and expenditure components, will be used.

Table 7.2 can summarize the types of information to be used in the different accounting systems. Using this table as a reference, administrators can anticipate the information sources that will be used on different occasions. This is important as administrators need to know who in the organization can have access to what types of information.

Table 7.2. Types of Financial Management Tools and Their Informational Sources

Types of Accounting Systems/ Informational Sources	Petty Cash Management	Simple Bookkeeping	Financial Management
Agency	X	X	X
Revenues	X	X	X
Expenditures	X	X	X
Staff		X	X
Clients			X
Services			X

Identification of information sources. The following two dimensions examine the nature of information: (1) routinized information/ nonroutinized information; and (2) hard data that are easily quantifiable and soft data that involve human judgment calls.

Agency data, revenue data, and expenditure data are quite quantifiable. Agency data includes data that will provide an identity to an agency, such as an agency code. It may also contain agency-specific information such as the year in which an agency was founded. The identity factor is important as staff members may work for more than one program in an agency. The information from these sources must be accurately presented and processed. However, the staff involved in providing services, the number of clients served, and number of beneficiaries are more difficult to define and measure. Judgment calls are involved. Because it is a question of judgment, the issue of whose perspectives and whose definitions will control looms large. The fact that it is also difficult to define services produces another problem.

Preparation of Data Dictionary

Informational Usage

Table 7.3 serves the following two purposes:

Data dictionary: This table serves as a road map for current and future users. Users are able to identify the variables that they use and their specifications. They should be able to understand the meaning of the codes from this data dictionary.

File/table organization: This table also provides a means of organizing data into different files or tables. This is one economic way of working with data. Often, if we make use of computer packages such as Statistical Package for Social Sciences (SPSS), we may not need to import the full set of data into the system. We need to import data that we need for the analysis at that moment in time. For example, when we want to analyze the trends of expenditures on office supplies we need information on the expenditures of items categorized as such; we do not need any staff information or service information.

Table 7.3 provides an idea of what files or tables should be utilized in analyzing the types of reports in Table 7.4.

If the types of information needs of each unit in the organization can be identified, the conclusion is probably reached that, while information on the aggregate number of service units may be updated by a department head, service information on individual clients may only be input by service providers who provide services for each client. A blueprint of the types of information stored in the system is probably one document that the administrators would keep. Easy access to knowing what information may be outdated and who should be responsible for updating it is one tool that administrators cannot forfeit. Table 7.3 provides an example of the way this information blueprint can look, in the form of a data dictionary.

Table 7.3. Data Dictionary of Financial Management Systems

Informational Source/ Name of Data Element	Location	Description	Format	Codes
Agency code	Agency	Codes for agency by department	A4	A001
Staff code	Staff	Codes for staff	A4	S001
Service code	Service	Codes for services	A4	V001
Client ID	Client	Codes for clients	A4	C001
Revenue code	Revenue	Codes for revenues	A3	R001
Expenditures	Expense	Codes for expenditures	A3	E001
Staff salary	Staff	Actual	N8.1	S002
Staff fringes	Staff	Actual	N7.1	S003
Monthly rent	Expense	Actual	N8.1	A002

Information Processing

In a computerized FMS, the user always grapples with building a system that is easily accessible to everyone and does not bring outrageous financial responsibility to the organization. As a result, it would be helpful for administrators to identify the types of reports that can be made accessible to the users on an ad hoc basis, which ones can be considered reactive or proactive types of reports, and which inquiries and periodic reports the computerized FMS generates. Timeliness in periodic information updating is more important for the reactive types of reports than for the proactive types of reports. Table 7.4 identifies which reports require information and where (i.e., in which files or tables) the information is stored.

Two types of reports are presented: reactive and proactive. Reactive reports are merely reports on activities, such as the areas in which monies are spent and the number of services offered. The proactive types of reports enable administrators to make projections as to the number of units of services needed.

Table 7.4. Financial Management Reports and Their Informational Sources

File Name/ Report #	Agency	Staff	Clients	Service	Revenue	Expense
RPT1	X				X	X
RPT2	X				X	X
RPT3	X	X		X	X	X
RPT4	X			X	X	X
RPT5	X				X	
RPT6	X	X		X		X
RPT7	X	X	X	X		
RPT8	X	X	X			
RPT9	X		X	X		
RPT10	X			X		X
RPT11	X				X	X
RPT12	X		X	X		
RPT13	X	X	X	X		
RPT14	X		X	X	X	X
RPT15	X				X	X
RPT16	X		X			
RPT17	X		X	X		
RPT18	X	X	X	X		
RPT19	X				X	
RPT20	X	X	X	X	X	X

Reactive Types of Reports

The following reactive types of reports enable administrators: (RPT4) to examine service utilization and service costs; (RPT6) to analyze the areas in which program efforts, such as staff time, money, and use of physical facilities, are concentrated; (RPT7) to assess the appropriate use of staff time with the number of services provided; (RPT8) to assess the use of staff time with the number of clients, individuals, or families served; (RPT9) to examine the number of services provided to clients, individuals, or families; (RPT10) to evaluate the costs of each type of service provided; (RPT11) to provide financial reports on a periodic basis, whether it is monthly, quarterly, or annually, on expenditures, as in the general ledger system; and (RPT12) to furnish service information on a periodic basis, whether it is monthly, quarterly, or annually, on units of services provided.

Proactive Types of Reports

The following proactive types of reports enable administrators: (RPT1) to identify problems in balancing the budget at the end of the fiscal year; (RPT2) to keep track of a runaway budget before a crisis occurs; (RPT3) to identify services that are overfunded or underfunded; (RPT5) to analyze trends of revenue-generating activities; (RPT13) to present service analysis reports to staff as a basis for common dialogue in setting service priorities on number of clients, individuals, or families served, number of each type of service provided, and areas in which staff time is concentrated; (RPT14) to engage the board of directors in reviewing the goals and objectives of an agency against the financial reports; (RPT15) to examine the trends of revenues and expenditures over a period of time, whether it is five or ten years; (RPT16) to evaluate the changes in the characteristics of clients who approach the agency in a period of five or ten years; (RPT17) to assess the service utilization patterns for a period of five or ten years; (RPT18) to facilitate an inquiry function with data provided by the FMS for administrators and designated staff members or persons on case- or group-specific information; (RPT19) to facilitate an inquiry function with data provided by the FMS for administrators, staff members, and designated persons on expenditures regarding budget items; and (RPT20) to provide an inquiry function with data provided by the FMS for administrators and designated persons on unit costs of each type of service. The designated staff person could be the supervisor of caseworkers who reviews case information or the caseworkers themselves who input case information for those cases for which they are responsible.

Step 7: Report Generation

The seventh step is the design of an information system that supports financial management.

Certain issues must be considered in the design of a computer system. Such a system should provide enough flexibility so that staff accessibility, information confidentiality, system maintenance capability, and user maneuverability can be attained. The computer system must take into consideration the following:

Fiscal and budgetary cycles. In this respect, we are referring not to the time of system design, but to financial management cycles. Fiscal calendars must be included in the system design. Other time issues include monetary contributions that must be used within a certain time frame, interest and dividends collected, services to be provided, and staff salary increments.

System maintenance. Often, administrators neglect the importance of system maintenance. By system maintenance, we are not referring to a maintenance contract on the hardware; we are concerned with the information in the system since it takes time, money, and commitment to set up an information system. We do not want to see information becoming obsolete or staff effort being wasted. Information in the system becomes quickly outdated if administrators do not factor in staff time and money in quality control and system maintenance.

Interface between computer function and human intelligence. Decisions need to be made on who has access to information. The dilemma arises when administrators ask for information from some staff members, but the same staff members may not have access to the information generated by the FMS. This is especially true with service-related types of information.

Unless staff members are committed and are diligent in providing case-related or service-related information, changes in the cases or changes concerning clients are not updated. This greatly affects informational relevancy and accuracy. But updating requires access. Another problem encountered by administrators is a political one: who decides who should have access to what information? This is a difficult question when administrators are talking about democratic planning and participatory management. The relational database allows data to be stored in different tables or files where the relationships among different data elements have been established.

The system should have enough flexibility that reports can be generated from information captured. A relation database is an answer. Documentation is vitally important. After all, people come and go in an organization. The transference of experiences and expertise must be preserved. Documentation of the data elements in the system (including a good description of the way data is collected, the codes used for these data elements, and forms used) is a necessary step in retaining human intelligence in an automated system.

System implementation. In Table 7.3, we presented a grid in which the persons and units responsible for providing the information were identified. Administrators need to implement an authority structure in which tasks are assigned to individual staff members. Administrators need to identify the persons who have expertise in handling types of information.

Step 8: Data Management

The eighth step is the specification of information processing. Since users' involvement is paramount in the design and the implementation of this system, identifying the importance of users' involvement is the first step and the determination of the extent of users' involvement is also important. Often, the accuracy of the information and the reports depends on the availability of the most updated information and the methods of computation used in report generation. For each report previously identified, a description is prepared of the data elements used and the ways computations are made. This document should be carefully disseminated to (1) those who generate the information for each of the data elements and (2) the prospective users. With this arrangement, problems associated with outdated information and wrong assumptions in the computations may be identified and corrected.

For example, in Table 7.5, staff members who provide multiple services should be consulted. Furthermore, it is also the responsibility of the administrators to provide training and orientation for the staff members so that the quality of the information to be collected is assured.

In Table 7.3, there is an example of the way data can be identified and organized in a data dictionary. Rather than describing all the data elements used in this FMS, there is a sample of data elements in Table 7.3. In Table 7.4, there are twenty reports. This is by no means all the reports an FMS can produce; these are some reports that support the four administrative subsystems. In order to generate each of the twenty reports, the types of information needed must be identified. Based on the types of information needed, the user creates data elements. Each data element should have at least a name, such as staff rank, with a code that can be recognized by the computer, such as ST005. This code is unique for this data element. Normally, a code should have no more than seven digits.

To follow this scheme, a list of data elements with names and codes is proposed as follows:

Description of data elements	Name of data elements	Codes
Staff code	ST001	(1) John Doe, (2) Mary Jones, (3) Caseworker 1, and (4) Caseworker 2
Service code	SR001	(1) parenting skill training, (2) day care, (3) counseling, (4) home care, (5) meals-on-wheels
Hours of services	SR002	number of hours, e.g., 2.5 hours
Hours of direct services	SR003	e.g., 1.0 hours
Hours of indirect services	SR004	e.g., 1.5 hours
Hours of supervision	SR005	e.g., 0.6 hours
Hours of administrative services	SR006	e.g., 1.0 hours
Date of services provided	SR007	e.g., 06/05/96
Number of families serviced	SR008	e.g., 3
Number of people involved	SR009	e.g., 15

Each staff member has a staff code. A 1 is put down for John Doe, the director, for staff code ST001; 2 is assigned to Mary Jones, the case work supervisor, for the same staff code. Then, 3 and 4 are assigned to the two caseworkers.

An example is: Mary Jones worked a total of 40 hours the week before data was collected. She spent 10 hours counseling clients (direct services) and 11 hours writing reports. Three of her 40 hours were spent on supervising her two staff members. In this case, staff code is ST002, hours of services (SR002) is 40, hours of direct services, counseling, (SR003) is 10, hours of indirect services, report writing, (SR004) is 11. Since Mary spent 3 hours supervising her two staff, SR005 is 3. Another example involves an agency in which parenting skills training, day care, and counseling are the three services provided; the administrators assign 1 for SR001 for parenting skills training, 2 for SR001 for day care services, and 3 for SR001 for counseling. If a parenting skill group session was conducted on 05/06/96 for 5 families with a total of 13 participants, SR001 will then be equal to 1, and one enters 05/06/96 for date of services (SR007) and 5 for SR008 for the 5 families served and 13 for the number of families served for SR009.

These codes will be used in Table 7.5, in computing which staff members are responsible for which types of services. For example, 2 can represent service provider (Mary Jones) and 10 hours for counseling services. Enter 3 for service code SR003 and 10 for the 10 hours spent.

After establishing the unit cost for the program, the user can generate a report such as the one shown in Table 7.5; such a report shows the number of hours each staff member put into a particular service. On the horizontal axis are the three service areas. On the vertical axis is information on the number of hours each service provider spent in each of the three service areas and the number of individuals or families served in each of the three areas.

For the computation, the assumptions used in the computation and the ways in which information is to be processed are spelled out. The following is an example of the way unit cost can be computed.

Table 7.5. Service Reports and Identification of Staff Involvement

Types of Services/Service Providers	Service 1 (e.g., group counseling)	Service 2	Service 3
Provider 1 (staff code)			
Average hours per week on this service			
Units served last month			
Provider 2 (staff code)			
Average hours per week on this service			
Units served last month			

Step 9: Computation of Data

1. Add all expenditures that are assigned to the use of this program.
2. For each of the items associated with that facility, compute:

    a. a prorated dollar amount based on (number of hours facility is used for this program ÷ number of hours facility is used for similar programs) × (months past in fiscal year ÷ 12) × (yearly total of expenditures on facility used)
    b. a prorated dollar amount for each of the items associated with facility based on (number of hours facility is used for this program ÷ number of hours facility is used for similar programs) × (months past in fiscal year÷12) × (yearly total of expenditures on that item)

The following paragraph describes the types of information generated by Report Number 7, which assesses the appropriate use of staff time with the number of services provided. Since, using the example provided previously, in conjunction with Report Number 7, it is known that a 1 for staff code ST001 refers to John Doe, 2 for Mary Jones, and 3 and 4 for the two caseworkers, the number of hours spent on each type of service by each worker can then be identified:

1. Staff number 1 to staff number 4 involved in the provision of such a service (staff codes)
2. For each of the staff members involved, average number of hours spent by that staff member on this particular service in that month (xx.x hours); average number of hours spent by that staff member on direct services, indirect services, supervising staff on that service, administrative duties; date of services provided (YYMMDD), number of participants (individuals), number of families served, and average number of beneficiaries in each family.

Computations: For each of the staff members who are involved in this service, perform the following computation. First, determine whether services are direct, indirect, or administrative functions, then compute:

average number of hours spent by that staff member on this particular service in that month (xx.x hours) ÷ average number of hours spent by that staff member on direct services, indirect services, and supervising staff on that service (xx.x hours) × (number of months past in this fiscal year ÷ 12)

On page 119, Report Number 8 refers to the use of staff time with the number of clients, individuals, or families served. After identifying the number of individuals and families served by each client, one can conceivably compute the total number of individuals and families served by staff members of a particular program.

For each case, we determine: (1) how many clients will directly benefit from receiving such a service; (2) how many clients are being contacted in an average month, and (3) the number of months that the case has been open, from which we can determine how many months the case has continued in this fiscal year. We multiply that number with the number of hours in an average month that client-worker contacts are made. This computation will give us the total number of client-worker contact hours.

For each case, we determine the number of individuals that benefit from such worker-client contact which is the number of beneficiaries for each case. We add up all the numbers of beneficiaries from similar cases. This will be the total number of beneficiaries for a particular service.

We add up the total number of client-worker contact hours for similar cases, and we come to results such as those in Table 7.6.

In reference to reports that are to be generated by the FMS on page 119, Report Number 9 computes the number of services provided to clients, individuals, and families. Table 7.6 provides a form in which such information can be collected. If considering another program in which three types of services are offered, namely, home care, meals-on-wheels, and recreational outings, 4, 5, and 6 can conceivably be entered, respectively, for service codes (SR001) for those services, since 1 has already been reserved for parenting skills training, 2 for day care, and 3 for counseling.

Table 7.6. Types of Client Systems by Types of Services Provided

Types of Cases/Activities	Home Care	Meals-on-Wheels	Recreational Outings
Number of client-worker contact hours			
Number of beneficiaries			
Number of cases			

In reference to Report Number 10 on page 119, this report evaluates the cost of each type of service provided. In order to compute the cost of each type of service provided, we determine (a) the number of hours spent by each staff member on this case, (b) the mean salary based on the current fiscal year, and (c) the money spent on the use of the physical building, utilities, etc. (see Table 7.7). (See page 119 for a further elaboration of this.)

The costs per case are determined by the following computations:

1. Staff costs on a case = the number of hours spent by each staff on the case × the mean salary of the staff
2. Physical space and utility costs = ?
3. Add the case costs of similar cases together to determine costs of each type of service.

In reference to Report Number 11 on page 119 one provides administrators with financial reports on a periodic basis, whether it is monthly, quarterly, or annually, on expenditures, such as the general ledger system; in Chapter 2, we mentioned that the types of reports needed affect the types of support that financial management is providing to administrators. In Chapter 3, we examined the types of accounting systems needed based on the degree of flexibility administrators have in spending and the amount of revenues or expenditures involved. We argued that not all costs need to be managed in a sophisticated FMS. Sometimes, a simple bookkeeping exercise can do the trick.

Table 7.7. Individual Staff Involvement in Each Type of Service by Hours Spent, Salary, and Other Indirect Costs

Service Code	Number of Hours	Average Salary	Space/Utility Cost
Staff #1 (staff code)			
Staff #2			
Staff #3			
Staff #4			

In Table 7.7, one makes reference to the four staff members that we mentioned on page 123. John Doe can be indicated by a 1 in staff code ST001; a 2 in ST001 is reserved for Mary Jones, the case work supervisor for the same staff code. Then, 3 and 4 are assigned to the two caseworkers.

Chapter 8

Applications and Exercises

This chapter helps the readers to apply the FMS framework along four dimensions: service appropriateness, service accountability, service effectiveness, and organizational efficiency. A good program is one that provides better services to needy clients and is efficient enough to maximize the work of the staff. In other words, administrators need to ensure that (1) the organization is providing the appropriate services to the right groups of clients, (2) the organization is managing the funds appropriately according to the funders and the board of directors, (3) the organization is spending monies to ensure clients are getting the services at the lowest cost, and (4) the organization is spending monies in a direction that helps to alleviate social ills.

ORGANIZATIONAL HEALTH

Step 1: Assessment of Organizational Health

The first step is to identify which administrative functions of the organization need to be supported by the FMS. Examine the existing state of the organization and determine whether it is operationally sound and which areas require some types of assistance. Some organizations are chronically dysfunctional and require a major overhaul.

Service-Related Assessment Criteria

1. What services have been offered to clients?
2. What indicators are used by administrators in determining that the right types of services have been offered to the right group of clients?

3. How much attention has been paid to ensure that the agency is providing the right types of services?
4. To what extent has the board of directors been involved in determining the types of services offered by the agency?
5. To what extent does the board of directors have knowledge of the types of services offered by the organization?
6. In what problem areas do workers have input in determining the operations of the agency?

Step 2: Identification of Problem Areas

Which areas of the organization can benefit from information generated by the FMS? Does the organization lack the capacity to, for example, make projections or forecasts in terms of its expenditures, caseloads, involvement with the community, needs for staff and expertise, etc.? Based on the identification of the problem areas, one can then assess whether the types of information generated by the existing FMS are adequate or whether the FMS must be redesigned to provide additional information.

Step 3: Identification of Informational Needs

Not all organizations require a high-capacity, on-line, information-rich FMS. The decision to have a sophisticated FMS may seem appropriate at first but it may prove to be an organizational liability a few years later. If the organization fails to provide adequate updating of the FMS, such a system may become a burden. Determine what information is needed by the organization in its present state in order to deal with some of the identified problem areas and whether there are financial resources to support such a system.

Fiscal Health Assessment Criteria

1. Based on an examination of the existing organization, which one or more of the administrative subsystems (i.e., service planning, service coordination, fiscal management, or program evaluation) requires support by the FMS?
2. Does the culture of the organization support the installation of an FMS?
3. Have staff been involved in fiscal management?

4. Have program costs been a concern for the administrators and staff?
5. Has the organization been providing services that are mandated by federal or state laws?
6. What proportion of staff time is spent in the provision of mandatory services?
7. What proportion of the organizational budget is based on monies that the federal or state government reimburses to the agency?
8. What proportion of expenditures is committed each year?

TAILORING THE FINANCIAL MANAGEMENT SYSTEM

Sometimes, the government tends to subsidize nonprofit organizations and confer upon them the responsibilities of performing planning, service provision, identification of community needs, coordination of other service providers, training of service providers, and evaluation of future service needs. Sometimes, a local agency is charged with assuming all service responsibilities. On one hand, this type of funding may lead to a smoother operation since the agency is held responsible in all these areas. On the other hand, the lack of competition leads to a monopoly of services. Therefore, it is important to examine what activities are expected from such an organization. Based on this assessment, one then can say what areas an FMS should support. Once one decides on the areas which the FMS supports, one can then examine how feasible it is to have this system incorporated into the organization.

Development of a Financial Management System

Three factors need to be considered: (1) the urgency of the implementation of an FMS, (2) the political support or the lack of support from participants of the organization, and (3) the types of financial resources that are made available for the implementation of an FMS.

After assessing an organization's health, one needs to examine the areas in which an FMS is likely to be supported. If the organization is in a state where funds management is in question one can expect that fiscal management will be the focus of the FMS development. If an organization is spending an enormous amount of staff time on service coordination, then the costs, the time spent by staff, and the number of parties involved in the service coordination process are important areas of information for administrators. If an organization is looking for new ground to break, question whether the organization is in a good position to expand. Expansion means planning and planning costs money. Another aspect of program planning is the types of services that are targeted to be expanded. Such an expansion is dependent upon the capacity to provide such services. One consideration is staff time; another is staff capacities. Before the organization computes the time needed to train staff, administrators may want to know whether the staff can be trained. If an organization is not providing the services to the right group of clients, one must evaluate which route the organization should take to make its services more appropriate. One must bear in mind that social services are not always welcomed by clients and that some clients are required to participate in some services in order to avert negative consequences. Many of the rehabilitative services fall into this category. Additionally, clients may be embarrassed to be seen in service centers. Even though the four administrative subsystems, namely service coordination, fiscal management, program planning, and program evaluation, are mentioned in this book, the development of an FMS must be weighed according to how much the organization needs to develop each or all of the four subsystems.

Political Support for Development of a Financial Management System

After assessing the areas that an FMS supports, one wonders how feasible it is to implement this system. Political support can be anticipated if the organization provides services that: (1) give the organization financial autonomy; (2) gain community endorsement; (3) are endorsed by workers; and (4) generate additional revenues for the organization.

Step 4: Identification of Services

Services that give the organization financial autonomy. In Chapter 1, we examined the development of nonprofit organizations, their evolution, their history, their missions, and the emergence of better financial accounting systems. The era of private charitable organizations has been followed by decades of publicly funded organizations. As funding sources have tightened their control on the ways monies are spent, some of the original functions of these organizations have been replaced by more measurable, more intangible, and more result-oriented services. The more measurable services are due to a need to measure costs and benefits.

Intangible services also obtain more attention as they save the auditors the trouble of attempting to quantify, to standardize, and to weigh human services in a rational manner. It is easy to wonder whether the failure of the auditors' attempts to quantify and to standardize is a reflection of workers' inabilities to articulate their work in measurable terms. In any case, as funding is weighed against some measurable and quantifiable services, some services which cannot be measured easily and which are considered somewhat secondary may be given little attention and fewer resources. After all, some human service organizations are established to provide an identity for some community residents. Some organizations are established to maintain social harmony. These functions are difficult to measure and so may be excluded from being selected as indicators of performance for these organizations. In 1977, private contributions accounted for 26.3 percent of the revenues of nonprofit organizations while in 1992 private contributions accounted for only 18.4 percent of the revenues of nonprofit organizations. In comparison, from 1977 to 1992, funds received by nonprofit organizations from the government sector increased from 26.6 percent to 31.3 percent (Hodgkinson and Weitzman 1996). Therefore, there is greater reliance by nonprofit organizations on government monies for support, and these organizations consequently restrict their activities to those that can be funded with government monies.

Services that obtain community support. Considering the concept of public good one must wonder whether the public has a say in the types of services that they need. Some services may be deemed more important to the community than others. Since a nonprofit organization requires support and endorsement from the community that it serves, how the community views the necessity of such services is a source of political power.

Furthermore, some organizations need collaboration from the community to be effective. The absence of community input deters program progress in both outreach and community participation.

Services that workers endorse. The design of any system without the endorsement of those who are charged with the responsibility of implementing it is somewhat handicapped because (1) the actual operation may not be well understood, especially when there are more workers who would like to see the system fail than those who would like to see it well implemented, and (2) the success of an FMS system depends on management of information. The accuracy of the information depends on those who provide it. The types of information needed by the FMS are related to: expenditures, revenues, services, clients, and staff time. The last three items require a fair amount of interpretation. Staff who are more committed to ensure the success of this system are likely to be those who pay more attention to the reporting of services that they offer and the time spent in the provision of such services.

Services that generate income. Services are important to an organization as income generated (e.g., service fees) provides the organization with the flexibility to increase staff's fringes and to promote a better image. Organizations that have greater flexibility in funds allocation are in a better position to grow and be innovative. Organizations that are restricted by the expenditures are likely to remain stagnant at best. Staff working for organizations having greater flexibility in funds allocation can expand their search for professional growth, while staff working for budget-constrained organizations would not have similar opportunities.

Service Provision Assessment Criteria

1. What services are mandatory for public funding?
2. How much staff time is spent on providing such services?
3. How much staff time is spent on providing other services?
4. What should be included in the financial management framework?
5. What does the FMS support?
6. How do dollars affect planning of services?

7. How do dollars affect case/service coordination?
8. How do dollars affect fiscal management and internal control?

Based on these considerations, administrators can obtain a some-what accurate picture as to whether an FMS can be introduced to the organization.

Step 5: Determination of Administrative Areas that the FMS Supports

The conceptualization of an FMS provides a framework for understanding how an FMS relates to the other subsystems. What information can administrators obtain from an FMS? How should administrators make use of the information generated by the FMS in administrative subsystems? These two questions will be repeated in each of the four administrative subsystems.

Step 6: Identification of the Types of Fiscal Accountability

Organizations that once relied on charity for survival met real challenges in the era of accountability. The first challenge came from the change from grants funding to contract funding. The second challenge came from collective fund-raising rather than individual fund-raising.

Grants versus contracts. Social service organizations used to receive grants for their expenses for the following years. A grant usually does not spell out the obligations that the agency must meet. The type of control for grant management is to ensure that the books are balanced. It is a documentation indicating that all monies are spent in areas that the administrators claim. However, the contract puts limits on the activities of the service agencies. Administrators of such agencies are likely to devote more resources to the provision of services included in the contract. Administrators are more likely to pay more attention to clients who are specified to be served in the contract since services under contract are reimbursable.

Collective fund-raising. Since funds were collected for social service agencies, agencies are required to substantiate their need of funds, the types of community support that they obtain, and the number of clients that these agencies serve.

Revenue Assessment Criteria

1. What proportion of funds is received from charity, from public funding, and from collective fund-raising?
2. What proportion of the funds comes from public monies?
3. What proportion of the funds comes from private donations?
4. What proportion of the funds is designated to be used for specific items, such as salaries, rentals, etc?
5. What proportion of the funds is assigned to administrators without any specific terms of usage?
6. What degree of flexibility does a program have in the area of funds allocation?
7. What types of services are contracted to be provided?
8. How many clients is the program supposed to serve?
9. How many units of services is the agency supposed to provide?
10. What are the patterns of funding and expenditures?
11. What are the types of services that workers provide?
12. Is staff involved in making decisions on the operating budget?
13. Is staff involved in the allocation of staff time?
14. How are funds audited?
15. What is the extent of staff involvement in the determination of fund allocation?
16. Is an effort made to monitor a match between revenues received and revenues committed?
17. How is the general ledger system used?
18. What is the proportion of fixed to variable income?
19. Is there a high or low volume of variable expenditures?

ADMINISTRATIVE SUPPORT

Key concepts involving the FMS's support of administrative decisions include the following:

1. Balanced budget
2. Continuous monitoring of funds

3. Accountability for sources and disbursement of monies
4. Forecasting of revenues and expenditures in the short term and in the long term
5. Determination of areas in which funds should be curbed
6. Determination of areas in which funds should be increased
7. Provision of a platform for staff to be involved in resource allocation
8. Provision of a rational sense of how resources should be allocated

COMPUTATION OF UNIT COSTS

This book provides a framework for an FMS. Through this system, administrators receive information in support of the four administrative subsystems, namely, program planning, service coordination, fiscal management and program evaluation.

The FMS offers methods of utilizing the information and provides some points and cautions in its application.

How can one make use of the FMS? Before analyzing how the FMS can support an organization, it is important to examine what the organization is trying to accomplish. This requires an examination of the goals and mission of the organization and whether such goals are clearly defined and identified.

Step 7: Examination of Organizational Goals

Goal formation is not as easy as it appears. To establish a set of viable goals for an organization is to establish guidelines for its operations and to set a direction for the years to come. In a competitive world, setting the wrong goals may diminish the value of an organization. Many social service organizations are still operating under goals that were set some thirty years ago. Realizing that some of the goals or mission statements are obsolete, one must wonder why administrators are not making the appropriate adjustments. One of the reasons is that administrators are more willing to be vague than to be wrong. Another reason is that both social policies that provide funds for these organizations and the communities that these organizations are designated to serve are as unsure or as uncommitted as administrators of the organization.

Step 8: Examination of the Activities of the Organization

If a big discrepancy in organizational goals and activities is encountered, one must ask whether the activities that are being carried out by the organization are necessary. At times, the assessment of an organization's performance does not reflect all aspects of work performed by staff. The next question is who is in the best position to know what activities should be included in performance assessment.

Organizational activities in a social service organization must be carefully analyzed and selected in this process. In the social service industry, agencies are criticized for being unresponsive to the needs of the clients and for spending too much time and effort addressing issues in areas where they can have little impact. Counseling, for example, may not be deemed important when there seems to be little impact on the lives of the clients and their families. One never asks what could have occurred if these clients or their families had not received the proper social and emotional support. Conversely, a lack of supportive services to desperate clients or families may lead to another form of criticism. The question involves how to strike a balance. In the absence of clearly defined goals and directions, it would be wise to consult with staff members who are being held responsible for client intervention. These activities are to be included in the FMS.

Identification of those responsible for carrying out the plan. Organizational activities are formally assigned to staff members or are contracted with other agencies. Such activities fall under the jurisdiction of the organization. Furthermore, these activities are the direct responsibility of the agency, and the organization is held accountable for staff performance.

Responsibility centers are individuals or units that are held accountable for the accomplishment of certain activities. Some of these individuals may be assigned to an ad hoc team in which members may come from different units of the same agency or from different agencies.

One must ask which organization is responsible for the work of what team and whether it is an ad hoc team formed on a temporary basis.

After identifying what activities are to be performed by an organization and who is to be held responsible for the completion of those activities, one must ask how much time is allocated by staff for the completion of those tasks. Time represents efforts, which can also be translated into monies.

Step 9: Assessment of Time Spent on Activities

After identifying the organizational activities to be measured, then determine (1) what portion of each staff member's time is allocated to these activities, and (2) what resources, such as physical facilities, utility costs, stationery, and phone costs, are allocated to each of the activities. Table 8.1 represents a way in which staff time can be designated in the performance of tasks.

Table 8.1. Computation of Staff Time Spent on Each of the Services Provided by the Agency

Service Code/ Staff Code	Service 1	Service 2	Service 3	Service 4	Total Staff Time (100 percent)*
Staff 1	35	35	35	35	140
Staff 2	35	70	35	0	140
Staff 3	140	0	0	0	140
Staff 4	0	70	70	0	140
Total	210	175	140	35	560

*Based on 140 hours per month

Time frame in service provision. It is always difficult to determine how much time one should spend on a particular task, especially if administrators, supervisors, and supervisees have trouble determining the scope of worker involvement and the types of client-worker cooperation anticipated. At the time of intake and when workers spend time with clients determining a service contract, the exact number of hours of contact is hard to determine. This fact may not mean it is a process that should not be monitored.

Rather, it means that such a determination should (1) build in some feasibility, informed by those who understand the process and those who have experience in handling similar situations, and (2) be reviewed and revised occasionally and accordingly.

Definitions of *direct* and *indirect costs* should be differentiated. Personnel costs are costs of time spent by staff on a particular activity. These costs include staff salaries and fringe benefits, such as medical and dental benefits and vacation days. Indirect costs include travel expenses, travel time allocated, use of physical facilities, use of telecommunications apparatus, stationery and other office supplies, and use of equipment.

Making comparisons of workers *performing similar tasks* is a strategy. It requires consideration of factors that could affect worker performance, such as client cooperation; the number of problems presented to workers to be solved; the vulnerability of the clients and their families in handling such problems; and the types of support clients receive from their families, friends, and neighbors. If these conditions are different, it should be determined whether a time frame can be objectively assigned for two workers handling two clients of drastically different conditions even though both clients may ask for the same services.

In Table 8.1, there are four staff members in a particular agency, which offers four types of services. Each one of the staff members was asked to put down the amount of time that he/she spent in each service area in the previous month.

In row one, assume that Staff 1, identified as John Smith, earned an annual income of $35,000. John reported that he spent his time equally in these four service areas. One can imagine that the agency expects each of the staff members to work thirty-five hours a week. Based on this, we have the information recorded in Table 8.1, which tells the readers that one staff member spent thirty-five hours each week divided equally among the four service areas identified. Another staff member, named Staff 3, worked in only one service area.

Table 8.2 allows identification of service areas that involve more than one staff member in the provision of services. Furthermore, the use of this table can provide information on the amount of time spent by agency staff in each of the service areas.

Table 8.2. Computation of Costs of Staff Time on Each of the Budgeted Items by Program (Line Item Analysis)

For Program 1:

Staff Code/Costs	Staff 1	Staff 2	Staff 3	Staff 4	Total
Direct					
Salaries					
Fringes					
Vacation time					
Indirect					
Travel expenses					
Travel time					
Use of telecommunications					
Stationery and office supplies					
Utilities					
Use of equipment					
Other					
Total					

Repeat the same process for Programs 2, 3, and 4.

Since this information is recorded on a monthly basis, one can examine the time spent by staff members in each of the service areas over the course of one year. There may be services that are more frequently requested in some months than in others. There may be areas in which service requests are on the rise or on the wane. This input can provide important programmatic information for administrators to plan for services.

After considering the time spent by workers on each type of service, one can see the costs associated with time spent. Based on the amount of time spent on a particular task and the related expenses, the program costs can be computed.

In Table 8.2, one can begin to compute the costs of staff involvement in a program. For example, assume that Staff 1, identified as John Smith, had an annual salary of $35,000 or $2,916.67 per month. Based on John's income and the number of his dependents, the agency had to put aside money for John's fringes, which are computed to be 22 percent of his salary. After performing the computation, the agency had to put aside $7,700 a year for John's fringes or $641.67 per month. Based on John's seniority and the position that he occupied, John was entitled to four weeks or twenty-eight days of vacation each year. In other words, the agency had to put aside $2,684.93 (computed by the formula [28 ÷ 365] × [$35,000]) for John's vacation time each year, or $223.74 per month.

In brief, the agency needs $45,384.93 ($35,000 + $7,700 + $2,684.93) each year to provide salary + fringes + vacation days for John. One can then compute that the agency needs $3,782.08 for John to cover the aforementioned items each month.

Assume that Staff 2, identified as Jane Smith, had an annual income of $40,000 and her fringes amounted to 20 percent of her annual income. Jane had the same four weeks of vacation time. The agency needs to put aside $51,068.49 each year, or $4,255.70 each month for Jane.

Furthermore, assume that Staff 3, identified as Mary Jones, had an annual income of $36,000. Mary's fringes were 15 percent of her annual income and Mary was entitled to twenty vacation days a year. The agency needs to put aside $43,372.60 a year, or $3,614.40 a month.

Staff 4, identified as Mary Doe, had an annual income of $24,000. Mary's fringes were 15 percent of her annual income and Mary was entitled to twenty vacation days a year. The agency needs to put aside $29,915.00 a year, or $2,409.60 a month.

Computation of Indirect Costs

Travel Expenses

In Table 8.2, the agency may subsidize $2,000 for John's travel expenses for attending conferences or meeting with out-of-state clients. One must remember that the $2,000 is not evenly distributed over the twelve-month period. The amount may subsidize John on one or two occasions. It would be simple for administrators to record the actual amount subsidized by the agency in the months in which they occurred.

Other Indirect Costs

Types of indirect costs include expenditures for telecommunications and equipment uses, utilities, and office supplies. It may not be difficult for an agency to determine the cost of each staff member's phone calls and photocopying. It may be more difficult to determine how much staff members contribute to the utility bills. The one concern that administrators should have is: whether it is possible to keep track of individual staff expenses without imposing excessive monitoring and control.

If that is the case, it would be simpler to divide the monthly telephone and utilities bills evenly among the number of staff members. If this is the approach, then divide the monthly telephone bills, say, $540, evenly by four staff members. Each of the four staff members would bear telephone costs of $135 for that particular month. By the same token, divide the stationery and office supplies of $680 into four equal parts, with each staff member bearing a cost of $170 for that particular month. Repeat the same process with Programs 2, 3, and 4.

COMPUTATION OF PROGRAM COSTS

The computation of program costs provides information to administrators on the areas in which resources are spent. After obtaining the information, administrators must decide what changes need to be made within the organization. In some areas, administrators may decide to put in more resources based on the oversubscription of services. In other areas, administrators may decide to curb the amount of time spent by professional staff upon realizing that most of the services requested do not require professional judgment or expertise.

Step 10: Computation of Program Cost

Table 8.3 presents a scheme in which the costs of the programs can be divided by the four services in accordance with the amount of staff time spent in the delivery of each of these four services.

Table 8.3. Computation of Program Costs on Each of the Budgeted Items (Line Item Analysis by Program)

Program 1:

Service Code/Costs	Service 1	Service 2	Service 3	Service 4	Total
Direct					
Salaries					
Fringes					
Vacation time					
Indirect					
Travel expenses					
Travel time					
Use of telecommunications					
Stationery and office supplies					
Utilities					
Use of equipment					
Other					
Total					

Repeat the same process with Programs 2, 3, and 4.

Based on information provided in Table 8.1, the amount of time each staff member spent on each of these four services is known. With this information, the direct costs, which include staff salaries, fringes, and vacation time, can then be computed. Indirect costs are computed based on information obtained in the Indirect Costs section.

COSTS OF SERVICE COORDINATION

Why is service coordination so important? In social service agencies, services to clients are products. The quality of the products is dependent upon (1) whether staff has the time for clients, and (2) whether the clients have problems for which workers can provide assistance within a prescribed period of time. In service organizations, services are specialized, and workers are responsible to provide a particular type of service. No one worker is responsible for the functioning of the individuals or the client families. Some workers are entrusted with the responsibility of providing whatever services that they feel are appropriate for their clients. Some workers must report and document the types of assistance that they render to their clients. Some agencies have documentation on operating guidelines and procedures; some agencies rely on the professional judgment of their workers. Therefore, one must ask what type of service coordination is needed by the agency and what kind of service coordination in the form of supervision is seen in the organization.

Service Coordination Assessment Criteria

1. What types of supervision are currently employed by the agency?
2. What types of work performed by the workers account for agency performance?
3. Do workers have the jurisdiction to provide services in collaboration with workers of other agencies?
4. What are the criteria used in establishing service eligibility?
5. What are the criteria used in the selection of clients?
6. What is the frequency of administrator-worker contacts?
7. Can the agency provide services solely by reliance on its workers rather than by also having to rely on the cooperation of other workers?
8. What types of power do the workers possess in making decisions in case-related matters?
9. How much time is spent by supervisors in case supervision?

Table 8.4 presents a scheme for determining which types of activities are decided by administrators alone or by a joint effort between administrators and workers. It also permits identification of areas in which input from staff is needed and yet staff has not been given the power to make any input.

Table 8.4. Types of Activities by Responsible Parties

Determined by	Workers Alone	With Administrators	With Other Workers
Case-related			
Service eligibility			
Client involvement			
Program budgets			

DETERMINATION OF SERVICE NEEDS

The following are steps required to determine service needs:

1. Establishment of the types of services which require extensive staff collaboration and those requiring little staff collaboration.
2. Establishment of the decision-making power between supervisors and supervisees.
3. Identification of the areas in which extensive staff collaboration is needed and yet no formal linkages are established.
4. Identification of the areas in which the decision-making power is divided between the supervisors and the supervisees and yet no supervisory structure is established.
5. Identification of the areas in which staff time is extensively used and yet staff has no input on resource allocation.
6. Assessment of staff time and costs for service coordination, and of the way time and costs are broken down by: direct client-worker time and costs, indirect costs by workers, and different types of cases.
7. Determination of whether service coordination requires linkages of workers from the same agency or with workers from other agencies.

Another area in which administrators need information is in assessing whether it is less time consuming and less complicated in service coordination if all tasks are provided by members of the same organization. Sometimes, workers are frustrated when they have to wait for someone else to make a decision. Sometimes, the decisions are made by people outside the organization. In these situations, workers would have no jurisdiction or avenues for questioning how and when decisions are made. Thus, worker performance will be affected by factors in addition to worker attributes or those of their clients. The organization, by making provisions to facilitate more effective services, affects service outcomes.

In this respect, administrators need to explore some mechanisms of providing better services rather than searching for more administrative controls or more ways of supervising staff activities. But making changes in the organization involves funds as it requires resources, in terms of staff time and staff expertise; it also takes courage as any resource redistribution signals political upheaval. Striking a balance among what is needed to make such a change, what changes would be made in the structure of the organization, and what impact it should have on staff morale and social relationships is a skill required of administrators. But what are skills without information? Information can be provided by the FMS.

PROGRAM PLANNING

Program planning requires an assessment of the types of policy changes, the types of changes in the clients' needs, the types of service demands a community makes on the agency, the types of training required by the staff, and the degree of program flexibility that an agency has in modifying the service delivery model.

Step 11: Direction of the Organization

Types of policy changes. One needs to know what policies affect the operation of the program. Any changes in policies that affect coverage for the clients or the types of services that the agency is charged with providing to the target population affects the operations of the organization and the performance of its workers. The earlier administrators can detect the types of changes in the policies, the easier it will be for them to devise changes to combat such challenges and lessen the degree of impact those changes will have on the target population. The more information administrators possess regarding these changes, the more accurate they will be in predicting the types and the quantities of such services. The more accurately administrators predict the services requested, the easier it will be for them to predict the number of workers needed to provide such services. In other words, forecasting of the amount of monies to be received in the forthcoming years, of the amount of expenditures anticipated by the organization, of the number of service units required, and of the number of service hours to be provided by the workers affects the types of programs that the organization plans and develops for the future.

Changes in clients' needs. For a social program to be responsive to the needs of the clients, the organization must be in a position to make changes and adapt to the needs of clients and the community. When one examines the evolution of these social programs, one probably comes to a conclusion that some of these agencies were charged with a mission to formulate service plans with their local community constituents so that services could be tailor-made to the local needs. How can an organization be involved in planning unless it keeps abreast of the changing needs of its clients and those of the community?

Types of service demands and types of training for staff. Based on the identification of clients' needs, one can design programs that would address those needs. For a program to address the needs of the clients, one needs staff expertise and staff time. The first requires training; the second requires resource allocation. The computation of the unit service costs helps administrators in formulating what services are needed, with their anticipated cost. This information provides a rational basis for resource allocation; it also enables administrators to establish the direction of the organization.

Degree of program flexibility. How flexible should the program be? The answer to this question lies within the mission of the program. Some programs are set up with vague and unspecified goals so that these programs can exercise their innovative strategies. This is the form of local programming that resulted in decentralized planning and block grants administration in the 1960s through the present. Decentralized planning works if these programs spend some effort in working with the communities. But working with the communities takes time and monies. Two problems occur if monies and time are not available. Without any monetary incentives, some programs may deposit more effort in areas which can either generate income (as in fee-paying services) or obtain reimbursement from government grants. If this is the case, some programs may have forgotten that they have an important mission in the establishment of such a program. They may not be reaching out to deal with the changing needs of the community. The second factor is time. If time is not spent working with the community, little effort may be spent on incorporating family members, friends, and neighbors into service provision. But the strengths of some social programs lies with the ability of the workers in drawing social support from those groups. Therefore, administrators should examine what services are being offered by their agencies and what services are being left out. After identifying the types of services left out, they may want to examine whether their programs can still be considered community-based. If some of the neglected functions would jeopardize the image, administrators may want to revisit what they need to provide and how much money it is going to cost the programs.

Program Planning Assessment Criteria

1. What are the changing policies that affect the program's operations and procedures relating to service eligibility, contracts with clients, duration of services, or types of worker input?
2. Who are the clients being served by the agency?
3. What are the types of service needs?
4. What are the types of services provided?
5. What is the impact of a particular service on the lives of the individual clients?
6. What types of expertise are required to provide the needed services?
7. Do the workers in the organization possess such expertise?
8. What is the direction that the organization should take in the next year, in the next three years, and in the next five years?
9. What service areas need to be expanded?
10. What service areas need to be terminated?

11. For each of the service areas that needs to be expanded, what types of political support or political opposition are the board of directors, the community, the funding sources, and the staff likely to provide?
12. For each of the service areas that are to be terminated, what types of political barriers may come from the board of directors, from the staff, and from the clients?
13. What is the extent of staff involvement in service planning?
14. What is the frequency of planning sessions with staff?
15. In which content areas was the staff involved in the planning sessions (including staff recruitment, service needs, community response to the agency, and policies affecting agency funding)?
16. To what extent was staff involved in program development?
17. What is the degree of staff participation in the planning process?

Table 8.5 provides a scheme to identify the extent of staff involvement and the types of information required for staff to participate in four areas in program planning, namely, budgetary allocation, service determination, assessment of clients' needs and service eligibility, and the types of support that the community requires.

Information obtained from answering the previous assessment criteria questions enables one to determine the types of program planning which can support administrative decisions in service planning, service expansion, service elimination, staff allocation, target population determination, and the degree of staff involvement in this planning process (see Table 8.6).

Table 8.5. Assessment of Types of Program Planning Needed by the Organization

Staff Capacity/ Program Areas	Information Availability	Information Needs	Staff Participation
Budgetary allocation			
Service determination			
Client determination			
Community assessment			

Table 8.6. Program Planning by the Degree of Staff Time Spent

Program Changes/ Staff Time Involved	Long-Term	Long-Term	Short-Term	Short-Term	Short-Term
Hours/Week	Program 1	Program 2	Program 1	Program 2	Program 3
Staff 1					
Staff 2					
Staff 3					
Staff 4					
New Staff 1					
New Staff 2					
New Staff 3					

Service planning must be based on an assessment of the clients' needs and the types of services requested or utilized by clients. Based on this assessment of service needs, administrators must reexamine the current staff force in terms of the types of skills required to provide services that are not currently provided, the direction in which the agency is heading in the near as well as in the distant future, and the types of resources required. In other words, service planning must involve an examination of the types of demand for services that would be placed on the organization and an assessment of what skills and resources are required for an organization to provide such services. Administrators need to assess whether moving in the direction of attempting to meet such demand for services is appropriate in the immediate or near future.

1. Forecasting capabilities of revenues, expenditures, service demands, service utilization, and staff capability and effort
2. Long-term versus short-term
3. Recruitment, training, and orientation
4. Resources
5. Services
6. How much input from staff, community, and clients

Continuing with Step 11, one must examine the forces at play in the organization. Based on this examination, one should be able to (1) identify the types of challenges encountered by administrators that need to be addressed in the next six months, (2) identify the types of changes to be made by the organization in the years to come, and (3) prioritize the long-term and short-term activities that the organization needs to undertake in the next three years.

Once this examination is complete, one needs to develop strategies to implement the plan, whether long-term or short-term in nature. The success of an implementation depends on whether the right people are assigned to the right tasks. For each of the activities identified, determine the person(s) who should be responsible for performing it, the average number of hours that each person needs to spend in performing each of these activities, and the types of benefits that each of these activities can yield to the clients or to the agency. Furthermore, for each of the activities, examine whether the organization has experience in performing it.

Based on this information, one should ask whether the activities identified by the organization can be classified as (1) an expansion of existing services, which means that one can expect the number of service units to rise, (2) a substitution of one service for another, which means that the number of units of one service will rise while the number of units of another service will decrease, (3) an elimination of one service, or (4) the creation of one service.

Based on the information provided in Tables 8.1 and 8.2, it is possible to derive the unit cost for a particular type of service as in Table 8.3. Using the information in Table 8.1, one can determine how much money the agency was paying for the amount of staff time spent on a particular service. For example, one knows that based on 140 hours spent at work by each staff member each month, Staff 1 worked on all four services evenly. Therefore, Staff 1 spent 35 hours on Service 1. Staff 2 spent one-quarter of the working time on each of Services 1 and 3 and half the work time on Service 2; therefore, Staff 2 spent 35 hours on each of Services 1 and 3 and 70 hours on Service 2. Staff 3 spent all of the 140 hours on Service 3. Staff 4 split the time evenly between Services 2 and 3; therefore, Staff 4 spent 70 hours on each of Services 2 and 3.

EXERCISE IN COMPUTATION
OF DIRECT SERVICES

Service 1—Travel Expenses: As Table 8.2 illustrates, the agency subsidized $2,000 for John's travel expenses for attending conferences or meeting with out-of-state clients. One must remember that the $2,000 is not evenly distributed over the twelve-month period. The amount may subsidize John for one or two trips. It would be simple for the administrators to record the actual amount subsidized by the agency in the months in which these events occurred.

For simplicity, Staff 3 went to a conference and the travel expenses amounted to $600 for that month. Since Staff 1 spent 35 of the 140 hours providing services in Service 1 area and Staff 3 spent all of the 140 hours in Service 1 area, the amount that should be charged to Service 1 for staff travel expenses is $500 for Staff 1 and $600 for Staff 3. The total amount spent was computed to be $1,100.

Service 2: The amount that would be charged in the Service 2 area is $500 for Staff 1.

Services 3 and 4: $500 was charged in both Services 3 and 4.

Other Indirect Costs

There are two methods of calculating the indirect costs for expenses such as telecommunications, utilities, stationery and office supplies, and equipment use.

Method A

Assuming that each service program bears the same amount of costs, one can compute the following costs for each of the service areas.

One month's telecommunications fees for the agency were $540; stationery and office supplies were $680; and the utilities amounted to $1,600. Therefore, the combined indirect expenses were $2,820, with each of the four service areas charged $705 for that month. This computation is based on an assumption that each of these four service areas expends the same program effort.

Method B

Assuming that the indirect costs should be in proportion to the direct costs associated with the amount of staff time invested in a particular service area, one can perform the following computation: divide the total indirect expenses (i.e., $2,820, derived in Method A) in proportion to the amount of staff time invested in each of the four service areas. For example, the combined staff time spent on Service 1 was 210 hours out of the total 560 hours. The amount charged to Service 1 is computed to be $(210 \div 560) \times 2,820 = \$1,057.50$. Similarly, $(180 \div 560) \times \$2,820 = \$906.43$ was charged to Service 2; $(135 \div 560) \times \$2,820 = \$679.82$ was charged to Service 3; and $(35 \div 560) \times \$2,820 = \$176.25$ was charged to Service 4.

EXERCISE IN COMPUTATION OF STAFF TIME ON EACH TYPE OF SERVICE

Step 12: Computation of Unit Cost by Program

Total costs for each program can then be computed. The total program costs should be the sum of direct costs (such as staff time and travel expenses) and indirect costs (such as telecommunications, utilities, and stationery and office supplies).

The computation of the unit costs involves the following procedures:

1. For each program compute the total costs of all services where the budget of each service can further be broken down into direct expenses (which includes salaries, fringes, vacation time) and indirect expenses (which includes travel expenses, use of telecommunications monies, use of stationery and office supplies, use of utilities, and use of equipment).
2. Determine the number of clients served. For example, if Service 1 is counseling to dysfunctional families, determine whether to use the number of families or the number of indi-

viduals as units of service. Another way of determining service units is a count of the number of worker-client contact hours.

3. After determining the expenses for each service in (1) and the number of service units in (2), a simple division of the amount of money spent on each service area by the number of service units would provide the unit cost for each unit of Service 1. Table 8.3 demonstrates how the costs of each service area can be broken down. The column totals indicate how much money is spent on salaries, fringes, and vacation time. The row totals indicate how much is spent on each of the four service areas, namely Service 1, Service 2, Service 3, and Service 4.

SERVICE 1:

Direct costs from Staff 1 = (35 ÷ 140) × $3,782.08
Direct costs from Staff 2 = (35 ÷ 140) × $4,255.70
Direct costs from Staff 3 = (140 ÷ 140) × $3,614.40
Direct costs from Staff 4 = $0.0
Travel expenses from Staff 1 = (35 ÷ 140) × $2,000
Travel expenses from Staff 2 = $ 0.0
Travel expenses from Staff 3 = (140 ÷ 140) × $600
Travel expenses from Staff 4 = $ 0.0
Indirect costs (using Method A computation) = $705

SERVICE 2:

Direct costs from Staff 1 = (35 ÷ 140) × $3,782.08
Direct costs from Staff 2 = (75 ÷ 140) × $4,255.70
Direct costs from Staff 3 = $ 0.0
Direct costs from Staff 4 = (70 ÷ 140) × $2,409.60
Travel expenses from Staff 1 = (35 ÷ 140) × $2,000
Travel expenses from Staff 2 = $ 0.0
Travel expenses from Staff 3 = $ 0.0
Travel expenses from Staff 4 = $ 0.0
Indirect costs (using Method A computation) = $ 705

SERVICE 3:

Direct costs from Staff 1 = (35 ÷ 140) × $3,782.08
Direct costs from Staff 2 = (30 ÷ 140) × $4,255.70

Direct costs from Staff 3 = $ 0.0
Direct costs from Staff 4 = (70 ÷ 140) × $2,409.60
Travel expenses from Staff 1 = (35 ÷ 140) × $2,000
Travel expenses from Staff 2 = $ 0.0
Travel expenses from Staff 3 = $ 0.0
Travel expenses from Staff 4 = $ 0.0
Indirect costs (using Method A computation) = $ 705

SERVICE AREA 4:

Direct costs from Staff 1 = (35 ÷ 140) × $3,782.08
Direct costs from Staff 2 = $ 0.0
Direct costs from Staff 3 = $ 0.0
Direct costs from Staff 4 = $ 0.0
Travel expenses from Staff 1 = (35 ÷ 140) × $2,000
Travel expenses from Staff 2 = $ 0.0
Travel expenses from Staff 3 = $ 0.0
Travel expenses from Staff 4 = $0.0
Indirect costs (using Method A computation) = $705

Step 13: Development of a Strategic Plan

It is important to set realistic goals for an organization. It is equally important to set realistic operational guidelines. How would one know what is realistic? In Chapter 1 is a discussion of the difficulty of assigning a dollar value to some social services. Some services benefit not only the clients who receive them but also society. Discussion was also focused on intrinsic values, such as clients' better adaptations to challenges in life and their better problem-solving capacities, rather than just the extrinsic values, such as improved financial situations. Strategic planning should be made with participation from the key parties, such as the workers and, to a great extent, the clients. At times, strategic planning is made by administrators in high offices without consultation with staff members, who are responsible for implementing such a plan.

How well can one predict whether the plan will be carried out accordingly? Two factors provide administrators with some indications. Administrators may have more confidence that their plans will be carried out smoothly if these plans are endorsed by their staff and that, if carried out successfully, they will bring greater prestige and authority to the organization, which would bring similar prestige and authority to those associated with the organization. In this respect, one should examine (1) whether these plans were formulated with support from staff members, and (2) whether these plans would provide benefits to the organization.

To what extent can one predict whether there are difficulties in implementing this plan? The assessment of this issue depends on whether support can be obtained from the staff. The support from staff depends on whether staff will see any gains from the changes in the direction of the organization. Staff members may be more supportive of a particular plan if they realize that the gains of the organization translate into benefits for them, in the forms of monetary gains or more prestige. The following areas need to be addressed: (1) for each of the activities identified, ask whether the activity was determined (a) by management, (b) by staff, or (c) with staff; (2) for each of the activities identified, ask whether the activity carries important political weight; (3) in program planning, determine (a) which activities are important for the organization in the near future or in the long term, (b) which activities are likely to obtain endorsement from staff members, and (c) which activities are politically significant for the organization; and (4) based on the types of activities that the organization is designated to perform in the next calendar year, ask what kind of budget is needed to carry out this operation.

Some of these planning activities are for the immediate future, say the next six months, which can be termed as short-term planning activities; some of these activities are long-term, which can be described as those which go beyond the six-month period (refer to the presentation made in Table 8.6). Administrators need to know whether staff has the time to be involved in the planning of the program. Often, social service programs are expected to be responsive to the needs of the community which they serve. Once the program is implemented, social workers are found reacting to clients' needs or community needs in an ad hoc unplanned fashion. As time goes by, planning is performed by administrators who are detached from the operations and social workers are constantly reacting to situations or policies in a disjointed manner.

Even though four service areas were identified in the previous tables, one must understand that not all service areas require planning. Some services are contracts between the government funding agencies and the service organization. The units of services, the scope of services, the amount of reimbursement and the method of operation are prescribed. For simplicity, one can ask the administrators of a program for the three important planning activities that each of the four staff members is asked to perform. Furthermore, as services may be provided in collaboration with other service providers, one can record the amount of time spent by staff members not originally identified in the analysis.

In Table 8.5, an assessment is made of the availability of information and the degree of staff participation needed to perform budgetary allocation, service determination, client determination, and community assessment. Once staff participation is identified as an important ingredient for performance of the tasks cited in this paragraph, the determination must be made of which staff in each program should be involved. In Table 8.6, administrators, having the capacity to oversee operations, should make an assessment of whether some staff should be involved in certain operations on a short-term or a long-term basis. Furthermore, administrators should also assess whether new positions are to be developed in the future to facilitate program development. Having identified the staff members who are "penciled in" in the organizational plan is a plan. The implementation requires staff cooperation. Table 8.7 provides a scheme for administrators to assess how implementable the plan is. This assessment is made on two dimensions: the first one is the degree of staff endorsement, and the second one is the importance of such an organizational change for organizational survival.

Step 14: Consider Budgetary Constraints

Any organizational plan made without considering the fiscal ramifications is only half a plan. One needs to (1) examine the types of monies received in the forms of "contract income," "donations," "fees," and "other sources" that the organization has been receiving in previous years, (2) determine whether monies to be received from various funding sources are expected to increase or decrease, and (3) determine whether the revenues expected exceed or fall short of the types of anticipated expenditures.

Table 8.7. Program Planning by the Degree of Staff Time Spent

Program Changes/Staff Endorsement	Long-Term	Long-Term	Short-Term	Short-Term	Short-Term
High/Medium/Low	Program 1	Program 2	Program 1	Program 2	Program 3
Staff endorsement					
Political significance to the survival of the organization					
High/Medium/Low					

Table 8.8 is an expanded ledger system that allows administrators to track monthly and year-to-date expenditures and match these expenditures against budgets allocated for each time in the general ledger system.

Table 8.8. Computation of Program Expenditures for Each of the Budgeted Items (Expenditures/Budgets By Program)

Program 1:

Service Code/Costs	Disburse-ments in Month	Year-to-Date Disburse-ments	Yearly Budgeted Figure	Projected Budget to End of Year	+/- Balance
Direct					
Salaries					
Fringes					
Vacation time					
Indirect					
Travel expenses					
Travel time					
Use of telecommuni-cations					
Stationery and office supplies					
Utilities					
Use of equipment					
Other					
Total					

Repeat the same process with Programs 2, 3, and 4.

PROJECTED BUDGET TO THE END OF THE YEAR

Table 8.8 tracks the amount of monies received and spent by the agency. This is the computation of the ledger system. In an earlier computation in Table 8.2, all the salaries and fringes of staff in the agency were added to derive the total salaries and fringes paid by the agency in the last month of operation. Table 8.9 illustrates how each expenditure in a budget will be tracked according to the disbursements in that month, the year-to-date disbursements, the yearly budget for that particular item, and the balance of the budget. This program expenditure form permits the administrators to examine which item expenditure is overspent or underutilized. Table 8.9 is a service-specific budget. For a program with, say, three service areas, three tables similar to Table 8.9 need to be prepared. This table provides information to make projections as to what kind of budget could be required for items overspent.

Year-to-Date Disbursements

The salaries and fringes of the staff from the beginning of the fiscal year can be added to derive this figure.

Yearly Budgeted Figure

This is the amount of monies anticipated. This figure is determined by adding all the contract monies that were promised to the agency for the full fiscal year. Add to this figure (1) monies that are expected from contributions, and (2) interest and dividends earned on the agency's account.

Monies from Contributions
for Agencies Experiencing Growth

If the amount of contribution monies for the agency were on the rise over the year, one may calculate the growth rate over a period of, say, five years. The amount of contributions for the current year will be calculated by multiplying the amount of contributions received during the past year by (1 + growth factor). For example, if the agency had

Table 8.9. Computation of Program Expenditures for Each of the Budgeted Items (Expenditures/Budgets By Service)

Service 1:

Service Code/Costs	Disburse- ments in Month	Year-to- Date Disburse- ments	Yearly Budgeted Figure	Projected Budget to End of Year	+/- Balance
Direct					
Salaries					
Fringes					
Vacation time					
Indirect					
Travel expenses					
Travel time					
Use of telecom- munications					
Stationery and office supplies					
Utilities					
Use of equipment					
Other					
Total					

Repeat the same process with Services 2, 3, and 4.

enjoyed a 7 percent growth rate for its contributions each year for the past five years, and the contributions received last year were $120,000, one can expect that the agency may receive a contribution that is equivalent to ($120,000 × 1.07).

Monies from Contributions for Agencies Experiencing Retrenchment

If the agency is experiencing a reduction of funds over the years, one needs to take special precautions. If the rate of decline in funds has gone from a negative growth of 2 percent five years ago and this negative growth rate has steadily escalated to 12 percent last year, one must wonder which negative growth rate reflects reality. Alternatives include (1) an average negative growth rate over the past five years, (2) a 12 percent negative growth rate, or (3) a higher than 12 percent negative growth rate.

Budget Projected to the End of the Year

One can project that the amount of monies received before the end of the year is based on (1) monies received, (2) monies committed, and/or (3) monies that can be expected under normal circumstances.

Monies received are simply an addition of all contributions. Monies committed are monies awarded in contracts and monies awarded by installment. Monies such as interest earned from accounts can easily be tallied. Monies from contributions and raffle ticket sales are difficult to predict.

The Balance Column

Each month, the FMS provides information to the administrators about the amount of monies projected to be received or not received and the balance between the amount of monies to be received and expended. This provides valuable information for administrators to monitor activities of the agency.

Based on the types of activities identified, determine (1) what methods are employed by administrators in ensuring that these activities are performed, (2) what methods are employed by administrators to ensure that expenditures do not exceed revenues, and (3) what service coordination is expected by staff members.

In the area of service coordination, one must explore (1) the number of staff members involved in service coordination and (2) the types of coordination activities involved. Even though each of the staff members is expected to spend thirty-five hours per week at work, one must wonder how much time each staff member spends counseling clients, writing reports, and engaging supervisors or supervisees in case conferences in a particular service area in comparison to the time spent on service coordination by calling other service providers or by written correspondence with various offices. In other words, the concern is whether staff spent excessive amounts of time coordinating services for clients rather than providing direct services to clients. As mentioned in Chapter 1, the service delivery model has become more complex as workers' activities have become more specialized. As a result, workers may spend numerous hours reporting services while the actual hours spent on establishing better worker-client relationships are reduced.

In order to explore the extent of staff involvement in service coordination activities, the identity of the staff who are involved needs to be established. A service area, such as Service 2, may need coordination between Staff 1 and Staff 2, as shown in Table 8.10. The cost of that service coordination may be quite different from another service area, say Service 4, which requires coordination between Staff 3 and Staff 4. This may be due to two factors: one is that Staff 3 and Staff 4 are staff drawing a higher salary than Staff 1 and Staff 2. Another factor is that Staff 3 and Staff 4 spend, on an average, five hours per week on the coordination of Service 4, while Staff 1 and Staff 2 only spend 2 hours per week in coordinating Service 2.

Table 8.10. Computation of Staff Time Spent on Each of the Services

Service Code/ Staff Code	Service 1	Service 2	Service 3	Service 4	Total Staff Time (100 percent)
Staff 1					
Staff 2					
Staff 3					
Staff 4					
Total					

Table 8.11 provides a grid for administrators to examine the number of workers employed in providing a particular service. As the number of workers involved increases, one must question

whether there was a need for workers to spend time negotiating and coordinating services. Table 8.9 presented earlier basically asks workers to report the amount of time that they need in working with others. Based on the information provided by these two tables, one can determine which service areas require extensive staff collaboration and the amount of time spent by staff. The information provides a basis for administrators to determine whether the agency should spend that much time in service coordination. Maybe it would be less expensive if some of these activities can be reorganized so that the amount of staff time spent in case or service coordination can be reduced.

Table 8.11 helps in identifying the staff members involved in each of the services provided by the agency. This table enables the administrators to compute the number of staff hours spent in performing particular activities and, consequently, the program costs. This computation provides administrators with a basis for determining whether or not activities with high program costs are needed and whether or not these activities require the involvement of all of the staff members currently engaged in such activities.

Table 8.11. Service Coordination Effort by Staff for Each Type of Service

For Service 1:

Staff Code	Staff 1	Staff 2	Staff 3	Staff 4	Total
Staff 1	X				
Staff 2		X			
Staff 3			X		
Staff 4				X	
Total					

EVALUATION OF PROGRAMS

Step 15: Evaluation of Program Activities

What information would administrators need for program evaluation? Evaluators are interested in exploring two areas: service effectiveness and program efficiency. Service effectiveness is a measure of whether the right types of services are going to the right groups of clients. Furthermore, it is an exploration of whether clients upon receiving such services are doing better as individuals or are functioning better at home or in their communities. Program efficiency is a measure of whether the programs are making good use of their resources so that staff time and resources are spent at an optimal level.

Program Evaluation Assessment Criteria

1. What are the characteristics of the clients receiving services?
2. What is the profile of clients receiving services?
3. What is the time lapse between service request and service receipt?
4. What is the amount of time spent by workers on clients?
5. What is the unit cost for each type of service?
6. What is the fluctuation of unit costs over the last three-year period?
7. Was the program planning appropriate?
8. What are the methods of service coordination?
9. How was the administrative audit conducted?
10. How many years did it take the agency to become established?
11. Has a new program or a new unit been established in the last twelve months?

Table 8.12 provides a scheme in which one can examine the types of services, the types of clients, and the types of evaluation criteria used in program evaluation.

Administrative Support for Program Evaluation

- Stage of development of the agency
- Types of evaluation
- Service-related
- Staff qualification evaluation

Table 8.12. Examination of Program Changes

Areas	Long-Term	Short-Term	Stages of the Program
Services			
Clients			
Staff			
Budget			

EXAMINATION OF PROGRAM CHANGES

Step 16: Examination of Changes Within an Organization

Some service coordination activities require the involvement of (1) specific staff members or members of staff teams, (2) cooperation among staff from the same unit or department in the same organization, (3) cooperation among staff members of different units or departments of the same organization, and (4) cooperation from staff members of different organizations.

Based on the persons involved in each of the service coordination activities and the number of hours spent by each staff member on service coordination, the costs of service coordination can be computed.

Based on the costs computed, one can then examine activities that carry high service coordination costs. An administrative decision needs to be made about whether such staff effort is worth the cost. Some judgment calls need to be made. That is, one needs to ask whether some activities are set as in-service training or as staff orientation activities.

In program evaluation, one also needs to ask (1) who will benefit from these services, (2) what benefits can be observed, and (3) what indicators are used in the measurement of such benefits (see Table 8.13).

Table 8.13. Computation of the Average Number of Clients Who Benefited from Each of the Services

Program/ Services	Program 1	Program 2	Program 3	Program 4	Total Clients
Service 1					
Service 2					
Service 3					
Service 4					
Total # Clients					

One also needs to assess whether the organization is performing what it was designed to perform. In this respect, it may be necessary to revisit Step 1. If all the benefits received by the clients are a product of activities identified in Step 1, one can expect that a successful completion of all objectives in Step 1 can translate into benefits for the clients. If there is a discrepancy between what tasks the organization has been established to perform, as indicated by objectives in Step 1, and the types of benefits received by the clients, it is possible that either (1) some of the benefits are not given priority by administrators, or (2) some benefits are not "factored in" in the measurement of performance.

Furthermore, one can calculate the number of dollars the organization spent on paying staff salaries, fringes, vacation days and the use of facilities such as utilities, stationery, office supplies, copiers, telephones, and fax machines for each of the service areas. Table 8.10 presents important information, that is, the number of services provided and the number of clients who received benefits from these services. Based on the monies spent and the number of people who received benefits from the agency, one can see the two sides of a cost-benefit analysis. The information provides administrators with a basis for determining whether services are effectively and efficiently provided. The examination of those who received services indicates whether services are going to the right group of clients. Utilizing the smallest number of staff hours to provide the same units of services is cost efficient.

Furthermore, comparison of the number of services provided and the number of clients receiving such services in each program provides a basis for administrators to determine whether some programs are more cost effective than others.

Bibliography

Altshuler, R. and Grubert, H. (1996). *Balanced Sheets, Multinational Financial Policy, and the Costs of Capital at Home and Abroad.* Cambridge, MA: National Bureau of Economic Research.

Antony, R.N. (1987). "We Don't Have the Accounting Concepts We Need." *Harvard Business Review,* 65(1), January-February, pp. 75-83.

Antony, R.N. and Young, D.E. (1984). *Management Control in Nonprofit Organizations.* Homewood, IL: Irwin.

Atkinson, A. and Stiglitz, J.E. (1980). *Lectures on Public Economics.* New York: McGraw-Hill.

Bane, M.J. and Ellwood, D.T. (1991). "Is American Business Working for the Poor?" *Harvard Business Review,* 69(5), September-October, pp. 58-66.

Berrington, A.C. and Kelly, A. (1995). "Expenditure Planning in the Personal Social Services: Unit Costs in the 1980s." *Journal of Social Policy,* 24(3), pp. 385-411.

Block, S. (1990). "A History of the Discipline." In Gies, D.L., Ott, S.J., and Shafritz, J.M. (Eds.), *The Nonprofit Organization: Essential Readings.* Belmont, CA: Wadsworth Publishing Company.

Borokhovich, K.A., Bricker, R.J., Zivney, T.L., and Sundaram, S. (1995). "Financial Management (1972-1994): A Retrospective." *Financial Management,* 24(2), Summer, pp. 42-53.

Bowen, W.G. (1994). "When a Business Leader Joins a Nonprofit Board." *Harvard Business Review,* 72(5), September-October, pp. 38-43.

Brunner, K. and Meltzer, A. (1993). *Money and the Economy Issues in Monetary Analysis.* Cambridge, MA: Cambridge University Press.

Bryce, H. (1978). *Financial and Strategic Management for Nonprofit Organizations.* Prentice Hall Business Reference Library, Englewood Cliffs, NJ: Prentice Hall.

Burch, J. (1991). The Case for Object-Oriented Financial Systems Development. *Financial and Accounting Systems,* 7(2), Summer, pp. 35-40.

Calderon-Madrid, A. (1995). *The Role of Private Financial Wealth in a Portfolio Model: A Study of the Effects of Fiscal Deficits on the Real Exchange Rate.* New York: Macmillan Press Ltd.

Cruthirds, T. (1976). "Management Should Be Accountable, Too." *Social Work,* 21(3), May, p. 179.

Drucker, P. (1974). *Management Tasks, Responsibilities, and Practices.* New York: Harper and Row.

Etzioni, A. (1975). *A Comparative Analysis of Complex Organizations on Power Involvement and Their Correlates.* New York: Free Press.

Feit, M.D. (1979). *Management and Administration of Drug and Alcohol Programs.* Springfield, IL: Charles C Thomas.

Filer, J.H. (1990). "The Filer Commission Report." (Report of the Commission on Private Philanthropy and Public Needs.) In Gies, D.L., Ott, S.J., and Schafritz, J.M. (Eds.), *The Nonprofit Organization: Essential Readings.* Belmont, CA: Wadsworth Publishing Company.

Francis, M.E. (1975). "Questioning the Validity of Social Accounting: Accounting and the Evaluation of Social Programs—A Critical Comment." In Seidler, L. and Seidler, L. (Eds.), *Social Accounting: Theory, Issues, and Cases.* Los Angeles: Melville Publishing,

Gies, D., Ott, S., and Shafritz, J. (1990). *The Nonprofit Organization: Essential Readings.* Belmont, CA: Wadsworth Publishing Company.

Harvey, P. and Snyder, J. (1987). "Charities Need a Bottom Line, Too." *Harvard Business Review,* 65(1), January-February, pp. 15-18.

Henderson, G.V., Trennepoli, G., and Wert, J. (1984). *An Introduction to Financial Management.* Reading, MA: Addison-Wesley Publications.

Herzlinger, R. (1994). "Effective Oversight: A Guide for Nonprofit Directors." *Harvard Business Review,* 72(4), July-August, pp. 52-60.

Herzlinger, R.E. and Krasker, W.S. (1987). "Who Profits from Nonprofit?" *Harvard Business Review,* 65(1), January-February, pp. 93-106.

Hodgkinson, V. and Lyman, R. (1989). *The Future of the Nonprofit Sector: Challenges, Changes, and Policy Considerations.* San Francisco: Jossey-Bass.

Hodgkinson, V. and Weitzman, M. (1996). *Nonprofit Almanac,* Table 4.2. Washington, DC: Independent Sector.

Holosko, M. and Feit, M. (1981). *Workbook for Internal Management.* Knoxville, TN: University of Tennessee School of Social Work.

Jacobs, V.K. (1990). "Tips on Building Consolidated Worksheets." *Financial Accounting and Systems,* 6(2), Summer, pp. 66-69.

Jones, R. (1992). "The Development of Conceptual Frameworks of Accounting for the Public Sector." *Financial Accountability and Management,* 8(4), Winter, pp. 249-280.

Jouvenel, B. (1968). "Notes on Social Forecasting." In Young, M. (Ed.), *Forecasting and the Social Sciences.* Social Science Research Council, London: Heinemann.

Knox, J. (1994). "Why Auditors Don't Find Fraud." *Accountancy,* 113(1206), February, p. 128.

Lohmann, R.A. (1980). *Breaking Even: Financial Management in Human Service Organizations.* Philadelphia, PA: Temple University Press.

Mayston, D. (1992). "Capital Accounting, User Needs and the Foundations of a Conceptual Framework for Public Sector Financial Reporting." *Financial Accountability and Management,* 8(4), Winter, pp. 227-248.

McLauglin, H.S., Radford, G.L., and Sullivan, T. (1990). "The Spreadsheet Market Now and in the Future." *Financial and Accounting Systems,* 6(2), Summer, pp. 21-27.

Merton, R.C. (1995). "A Functional Perspective of Financial Intermediation." *Financial Management,* 24(2), Summer, pp. 23-41.

Miller, G.J. (1991). *Government Financial Management Theory.* New York: Marcel Dekker, Inc.

Musgrave, R. (1985). "A Brief History of Fiscal Doctrine." In Auerbach, A.J. and Feldstein, M. (Eds.), *Handbook of Public Economics,* Volume 1, Chapter 1, pp. 1-59. New York: Elsevier Science Publishers.

Musgrave, R. (1988). "Public Finance in a Democratic Society." *Public Administrative Review,* 48(3), May, pp. 743-744.

Musgrave, R. (1990). "Reconsidering the Fiscal Role of Government." *The American Economic Review,* 87(2), May, pp. 156-159.

Newberry, S.M. (1995). "Accounting for Contributed Services: The FAB's Conceptual Confusion." *Financial Accountability and Management,* 11(3), August, pp. 241-258.

Newman, E. and Turem, J. (1974). "The Crisis of Accountability." *Social Work,* 19(1), January, pp. 5-9.

Organization for Economic Cooperation and Development. (1982). *Budget Financing and Monetary Control.* Paris, France: OECD.

Organization for Economic Cooperation and Development. (1995). *Budgeting for Results: Perspectives on Public Expenditure Management.* Paris, France: OECD.

Ott, A.F. (1993). *Public Sector Budgets: A Comparative Study.* Brookfield, VT: Edward Elgar Publishing Company.

Petersen, I.J. (1995). Budgetary Control of Hospitals—Ritual Rhetoric and Rationalized Myths? *Financial Accountability and Management,* 11(3), August, pp. 207-221.

Pinch, T., Mulkay, M., and Ashmore, M. (1989). "Clinical Budgeting: Experimentation in Social Service Sciences: A Drama in Five Acts." *Accounting, Organizations, and Society,* 124(3), pp. 271-300.

Rodgers, T.J. (1993). "No Excuses Management." *Small Business Report,* 18(12), December, pp. 65-68.

Rodwin, M.A. (1992). "The Organized American Medical Profession's Response to Financial Conflicts of Interest: 1890-1992." *The Milbank Quarterly,* 70(4), pp. 703-741.

Schesinger, L.A. and Heskett, J.L. (1991). "The Service-Driven Service Company." *Harvard Business Review,* 69(5), September-October, pp. 71-81.

Shadbegian, R. (1993). "The Fiscal Structure of the United States." In Ott, A.F. (Ed.), *Public Sector Budgets: A Comparative Study.* Brookfield, VT: Edward Elgar Publishing.

Skidmore, R.A. (1995). *Social Work Administration: Dynamic Management and Human Relationships.* Third Edition. Englewood Cliffs, NJ: Prentice-Hall.

Smith, M.T. (1992). "Giving Wisely: When the Need Is Great." *Money,* 21(12), December, pp. 114-117.

Stewart, G.T. and Graven, B.M. (1995). "Corporate Governance, Financial Reporting, and Cost of Containing the AIDS Threat to Scotland." *Financial Accountability and Management,* 11(3), August, pp. 223-239.

Taylor, F.A. (1990). "The Numerate Social Worker." *Journal of Social Work Education,* Winter, No.1, pp. 25-34.

Thompson, G.D. (1995). "Problems with Service Performance Reporting: The Case of Public Art Galleries." *Financial Accountability and Management,* 11(4), November, pp. 337-350.

Tyran, M. (1980). *Computerized Financial Forecasting and Performance Reporting.* Englewood Cliffs, NJ: Prentice-Hall.

United States Government. (1996). *The Economic and Budget Outlook: Fiscal Years 1997-2006.* May. Washington, DC: U.S. Government Printing Office.

Wagener, H.J. (Ed.). (1994). *The Political Economy of Transformation.* Physica-Verlag. New York: Springer-Verlag.

Yang, D.C. (1991). "The Added Control of Lotus Macros." *Financial Accounting and Systems,* 7(2), Summer, pp. 29-34.

Young, M. (1968). *Forecasting and the Social Sciences.* Social Science Research Council, London: Heinemann.

Index

Order Your Own Copy of
This Important Book for Your Personal Library!

FINANCIAL MANAGEMENT IN HUMAN SERVICES

_____ in hardbound at $39.95 (ISBN: 0-7890-0131-4)

_____ in softbound at $19.95 (ISBN: 0-7890-0569-7)

COST OF BOOKS_____	☐ **BILL ME LATER:** ($5 service charge will be added) (Bill-me option is good on US/Canada/Mexico orders only; not good to jobbers, wholesalers, or subscription agencies.)
OUTSIDE USA/CANADA/ MEXICO: ADD 20%_____	
POSTAGE & HANDLING_____ *(US: $3.00 for first book & $1.25 for each additional book) Outside US: $4.75 for first book & $1.75 for each additional book)*	☐ Check here if billing address is different from shipping address and attach purchase order and billing address information. Signature_____
SUBTOTAL_____	☐ **PAYMENT ENCLOSED: $**_____
IN CANADA: ADD 7% GST_____	☐ **PLEASE CHARGE TO MY CREDIT CARD.**
STATE TAX_____ *(NY, OH & MN residents, please add appropriate local sales tax)*	☐ Visa ☐ MasterCard ☐ AmEx ☐ Discover Account #_____
FINAL TOTAL_____ *(If paying in Canadian funds, convert using the current exchange rate. UNESCO coupons welcome.)*	Exp. Date_____ Signature_____

Prices in US dollars and subject to change without notice.

NAME _____

INSTITUTION _____

ADDRESS _____

CITY _____

STATE/ZIP _____

COUNTRY _____ COUNTY (NY residents only) _____

TEL _____ FAX _____

E-MAIL_____

May we use your e-mail address for confirmations and other types of information? ☐ Yes ☐ No

Order From Your Local Bookstore or Directly From
The Haworth Press, Inc.
10 Alice Street, Binghamton, New York 13904-1580 • USA
TELEPHONE: 1-800-HAWORTH (1-800-429-6784) / Outside US/Canada: (607) 722-5857
FAX: 1-800-895-0582 / Outside US/Canada: (607) 772-6362
E-mail: getinfo@haworthpressinc.com
PLEASE PHOTOCOPY THIS FORM FOR YOUR PERSONAL USE.

BOF96